Los Angeles Public Branch
Social Science/Philosophy
& Religion Dept.
630 W. Fifth Street
Los Angeles, CA 90071

WITHDRAWN

DEC 1 3 2005

W9-CKH-179

LIVING THROUGH | THE COLD WAR

LIVING
THROUGH THE
RED SCARE

Edited by Derek C. Maus

Bruce Glassman, *Vice President*
Bonnie Szumski, *Publisher*
Helen Cothran, *Managing Editor*
Scott Barbour, *Series Editor*

L.A. PUBLIC LIBRARY - SOCIAL SCIENCE/PHIL/REL

335.40973
L7855

IJAN 3 0 2006

GREENHAVEN PRESS
An imprint of Thomson Gale, a part of The Thomson Corporation

THOMSON
——✳——™
GALE

Detroit • New York • San Francisco • San Diego • New Haven, Conn.
Waterville, Maine • London • Munich

© 2006 Thomson Gale, a part of The Thomson Corporation.

Thomson and Star Logo are trademarks and Gale and Greenhaven Press are registered trademarks used herein under license.

For more information, contact
Greenhaven Press
27500 Drake Rd.
Farmington Hills, MI 48331-3535
Or you can visit our Internet site at http://www.gale.com

ALL RIGHTS RESERVED.
No part of this work covered by the copyright hereon may be reproduced or used in any form or by any means—graphic, electronic, or mechanical, including photocopying, recording, taping, Web distribution, or information storage retrieval systems—without the written permission of the publisher.

Every effort has been made to trace the owners of copyrighted material.

Cover credit: © Hulton Archive by Getty Images. A group of women protest the Soviet regime and the arrival of Soviet foreign minister Andrei Gromyko in New York in 1951.

LIBRARY OF CONGRESS CATALOGING-IN-PUBLICATION DATA

Living through the red scare / Derek C. Maus, book editor.
  p. cm. — (Living through the cold war)
  Includes bibliographical references and index.
  ISBN 0-7377-2915-5 (lib. : alk. paper)
   1. Anti-communist movements—United States—History. 2. Anti-communist movements—United States—History—Sources. 3. Subversive activities—United States—History—20th century. 4. Subversive activities—United States—History—20th century—Sources. 5. Internal security—United States—History—20th century. 6. Internal security—United States—History—20th century—Sources. I. Maus, Derek C. II. Series.
  E743.5.L57 2006
  320.973'09'045—dc22

                                                          2005046029

Printed in the United States of America

CONTENTS

Chapter 1: Building Up the Red Scare

Chapter 2: Speaking Out Against the Red Scare

Chapter 3: The Cultural Effects of the Red Scare

At the midpoint of the Cold War, in early 1968, U.S. television viewers saw surprising reports from Vietnam, where American ground troops had been fighting since 1965. They learned that South Vietnamese Communist rebels, known as the Vietcong, had attacked unexpectedly throughout the country. At one point Vietcong insurgents engaged U.S. troops and officials in a firefight at the very center of U.S. power in Vietnam, the American embassy in South Vietnam's capital, Saigon. Meanwhile, thousands of soldiers and marines faced a concerted siege at Khe Sanh, an isolated base high in central Vietnam's mountains. Their adversary was not the Vietcong, but rather the regular North Vietnamese army.

Reporters and U.S. citizens quickly learned that these events constituted the Tet Offensive, a coordinated attack by Vietnamese Communists that occurred in late January, the period of Tet, Vietnam's new year. The American public was surprised by the Tet Offensive because they had been led to believe that the United States and its South Vietnamese allies were winning the war, that Vietcong forces were weak and dwindling, and that the massive buildup of American forces (there were some five hundred thousand U.S. troops in Vietnam by early 1968), ensured that the south would remain free of a Communist takeover. Since 1965, politicians, pundits, and generals had claimed that massive American intervention was justified and that the war was being won. On a publicity tour in November 1967 General William Westmoreland, the American commander in Vietnam, had assured officials and reporters that "the ranks of the Vietcong are thinning steadily" and that "we have reached a point where the end begins to come into view." President Lyndon B. Johnson's advisers, meanwhile, continually encouraged him to publicly emphasize "the light at the end of the tunnel."

Ordinary Americans had largely supported the troop build-up in Vietnam, believing the argument that the country was an important front in the Cold War, the global effort to stop the spread of communism that had begun in the late 1940s. Communist regimes already held power in nearby China, North Korea, and in northern Vietnam; it was deemed necessary to hold the line in the south not only to prevent communism from taking hold there but to prevent other nations from falling to communism throughout Asia. In 1965, polls showed that 80 percent of Americans believed that intervention in Vietnam was justified despite the fact that involvement in this fight would alter American life in numerous ways. For example, young men faced the possibility of being drafted and sent to fight—and possibly die—in a war thousands of miles away. As the war progressed, citizens watched more and more of their sons—both draftees and enlisted men—being returned to the United States in coffins (approximately fifty-eight thousand Americans died in Vietnam). Antiwar protests roiled college campuses and sometimes the streets of major cities. The material costs of the war threatened domestic political reforms and America's economic health, offering the continuing specter of rising taxes and shrinking services. Nevertheless, as long as the fight was succeeding, a majority of Americans could accept these risks and sacrifices.

Tet changed many minds, suggesting as it did that the war was not, in fact, going well. When CBS news anchor Walter Cronkite, who was known as "the most trusted man in America," suggested in his broadcast on the evening of February 27 that the Vietnam War might be unwinnable and could only end in a stalemate, many people wondered if he might be right and began to suspect that the positive reports from generals and politicians might have been misleading. It was a turning point in the battle for public opinion. Johnson reportedly said that Cronkite's expressions of doubt signaled the loss of mainstream America's support for the war. Indeed, after Tet more and more people joined Cronkite in wondering whether fighting this obscure enemy in an isolated country halfway around the world was worth the cost—whether it was a truly important front in the Cold War. They made their views known through demonstrations and opinion polls, and politicians were forced to respond. In a dramatic and unexpected turn of events, Johnson declined to run for reelection in 1968, stating that his involvement in the political campaign would detract from his efforts to negotiate a peace agreement with North Vietnam. His successor, Richard Nixon, won the election after promising to end the war.

The Tet Offensive and its consequences provide strong examples of how the Cold War touched the lives of ordinary Americans. Far from being an abstract geopolitical event, the Cold War, as Tet reveals, was an ever-present influence in the everyday life of the nation. Greenhaven Press's Living Through the Cold War series provides snapshots into the lives of ordinary people during the Cold War, as well as their reactions to its major events and developments. Each volume is organized around a particular event or distinct stage of the Cold War. Primary documents such as eyewitness accounts and speeches give firsthand insights into both ordinary peoples' experiences and leaders' decisions. Secondary sources provide factual information and place events within a larger global and historical context. Additional resources include a detailed introduction, a comprehensive chronology, and a thorough bibliography. Also included are an annotated table of contents and a detailed index to help the reader locate information quickly. With these features, the Living Through the Cold War series reveals the human dimension of the superpower rivalry that defined the globe during most of the latter half of the twentieth century.

The term *Red Scare* has been applied to two separate periods of American history. The first usage refers to the years immediately following the Russian Revolution of 1917, during which the fear arose that the revolutionary sentiment that toppled the centuries-old Romanov dynasty in Russia might spread to war-ravaged Europe and even the United States. The second usage refers to the period between roughly 1947 and 1954, when Cold War crusaders such as J. Edgar Hoover and Senator Joseph McCarthy (R-WI) warned Americans about the hidden presence of Communists in the entertainment industry, the nuclear weapons development program, the government, the schools and universities, and virtually every other walk of life. Although these two periods are separated by more than twenty years, they were both fueled by the same underlying suspicion of radicalism, which existed since at least the second half of the nineteenth century. Both Red Scares can be attributed principally to an increased perception of crisis—due to World War I and the Russian Revolution in the first instance and the Cold War, with its dual threats of totalitarian tyranny and nuclear war, in the second—combined with opportunistic individuals willing to exploit such a sense of crisis to their political advantage. Although there is plentiful evidence of subversive activity in the United States during both Red Scares, the sad irony of both periods is that the hysteria they fostered tended to ensnare many more innocent individuals than guilty ones.

A History of Hostility

The Communist Party of the United States (CPUSA) was founded in 1919, but the antirevolutionary reaction of the late 1910s and early 1920s in the United States focused not just on card-carrying Communists, but also on Socialists, anarchists, labor organizers, and any other politically leftist groups believed to oppose the values of the nation. Members of labor unions such as the American Federation of Labor (AFL) and the International Workers of the World (IWW or "Wobblies") and leftist politicians such as Eugene V. Debs—who had received 6 percent of the national popular vote as the Socialist Party's candidate for the U.S. presidency in 1916—were accused of treason, often for little more than seeking to improve the working conditions in factories or voicing their opposition to World War I. Under the Espionage Act of 1917 and the Sedition Act of 1918, individuals could be arrested not only for actively opposing the United States, but merely for passing out leaflets that criticized American participation in the war. The philosophical roots of such widespread suppression of dissent go back several decades.

· The late nineteenth and early twentieth centuries were filled with strikes and violent clashes between owners and workers as the national economy was transformed from predominantly agricultural to urban and industrial. Major strikes in the railroad industry (such as the "Great Railroad Strike" of 1877 or the Pullman Strike of 1894), the mining industry (such as the Ludlow Strike of 1913–1914), and the steel industry (such as the Homestead Strike of 1892 and the "Great Steel Strike" in 1919) marked the fifty years of rapid industrialization following the Civil War. These strikes were frequently suppressed with brutal violence against the rebellious workers. Moreover, the organizers of such labor actions were routinely and mistakenly branded as "troublemakers" in the service of foreign Socialist or anarchist groups. Historians Richard Hofstadter and Michael Wallace note that the pattern of bloody reaction against strikers in the United States does not accurately reflect American labor's relative lack of political radicalism:

> The rate of industrial violence in America is striking in light of the fact that no major American labor organization has ever advocated violence as a policy, that extremely militant class-conflict philosophies [e.g., Marxist communism] have not prevailed here, and that the percentage of the American labor force organized in unions has always been . . . lower than in most advanced industrial countries.[1]

Although progressive political figures such as William Jennings Bryan, Robert M. La Follette, and Debs gained some notoriety, they were generally overshadowed by mainstream politicians who stood to gain more from the unprecedented economic growth of the time. When the Bolsheviks seized power in Russia in November 1917, their rallying cry of "Workers of the World, Unite!" triggered fears of a wider revolution in both Europe and the United States, which already had a track record of responding aggressively to labor uprisings.

The Red Scare of 1919–1920

The first Red Scare flared up most visibly in the mass arrests and deportations of 1919 and 1920. These so-called Palmer raids were carried out by the Justice Department under the leadership of Attorney General A. Mitchell Palmer and his deputy, J. Edgar Hoover, who would later head the Federal Bureau of Investigation (FBI) from 1924 to 1972. Perhaps the most infamous of these raids took place in December 1919, when Palmer's men rounded up 249 influential radicals, charged them under the Espionage and Sedition acts, and summarily deported them on a ship bound for the Soviet Union. Over the course of the next seven months, tens of thousands of union leaders, CPUSA members, Socialist politicians, and anarchists were arrested and often deported on the pretext of treason. Any hint of subversive intent could lead to grave consequences even if one was not caught up in the Palmer raids. For example, a pair of Italian anarchists in Boston, Nicola Sacco and Bartolomeo Vanzetti, were arrested for murder in 1920, convicted in a sensational trial during which the main evidence against them was their political affiliation, and executed after seven years of fruitless appeals. Sacco and Vanzetti became icons of antiradical fervor, and their execution polarized public and intellectual opinion. They were either revered as innocent victims of paranoia or reviled as reminders of the need for vigilance.

Despite worries about occasional "excesses" the Palmer raids initially met with great public approval. Palmer's ambition—he actively sought the Democratic presidential nomination in 1920—proved to be his undoing, though. Relying on sketchy evidence, he warned of a major Communist uprising in the United States on May Day (May 1) in 1920. When this failed to take place Palmer's credibility was irreparably damaged, and he soon faded from the scene. The anti-Communist sentiment that had helped Palmer rise to prominence remained, however, even though the public frenzy had subsided considerably by 1921. The peace and relatively widespread prosperity of the "Roaring Twenties" helped minimize the degree to which Americans felt threatened by revolution. Both the influence of radical groups and the opposition to them intensified, however, during the Great Depression, which lasted from 1929 well into the 1930s. Much as it had in the late 1800s and early 1900s, the opposition largely remained local—such as the mob that attacked a Communist-organized march by unemployed autoworkers in Dearborn, Michigan, in 1932—rather than being part of government policy, as was the case with the Palmer raids and the Espionage and Sedition acts during the first Red Scare. In fact, opposition to President Franklin D. Roosevelt's New Deal, a wide-ranging set of social and economic policies instituted in 1933, was frequently tinged with suspicions or outright accusations of communism.

The Origins of HUAC

One of the most prominent anti-Communist institutions in American history got its start during the 1930s. Representative Hamilton Fish (R-NY) convened a special committee in the House of Representatives in July 1930 to hear testimony about the gathering threat of communism. Hoover was among the list of witnesses who testified that the lack of attention paid to communism since the early 1920s had allowed it to regroup in the United States. The committee issued recommendations to outlaw the CPUSA and deport any foreign-born Communists living in the United States, but neither was accepted. Four years later, Representative Samuel Dickstein (D-NY) proposed another special House committee to investigate an alleged rise in pro-Nazi activity in the United States. When Congress approved his committee, appointing John McCormack (D-MA) as its chair, it widened the scope of its investigations to once again include

Communist propaganda. The Dickstein-McCormack committee heard five months of testimony in late 1934 but generally failed to expose any large-scale radicalism on either the right or the left.

By 1938 economic recovery was sputtering in the United States, and the prospects of war in Europe seemed increasingly likely. In this uncertain atmosphere a former New Deal advocate, Representative Martin Dies (D-TX), proposed and became chair of a committee intended to expose subversive elements in American society. Officially named the House Select Committee on Un-American Activities, it quickly acquired the oddly inaccurate acronym HUAC, by which it would enter the public consciousness. Although, like the Dickstein-McCormack committee before it, the committee initially was given the task of investigating pro-Nazi and pro-Communist groups and individuals, Dies quickly turned its focus to New Deal institutions such as the Federal Theatre Project, which he claimed was full of Communists. This incarnation of HUAC carried out highly publicized inquiries during 1938 and 1939, most of which seemed to implicate New Deal programs and American labor unions as either explicit or implicit allies of communism. When the Soviet Union and Nazi Germany signed a mutual nonaggression pact just prior to the outbreak of World War II in July 1939, the distinction between left-wing and right-wing subversion was essentially removed and the public strongly backed Dies's crusade against radicalism of all kinds.

Perhaps the most tangible result of HUAC's hearings in the late 1930s was the passage of the Smith Act (officially called the Alien Registration Act) of June 1940, which required all foreigners living in the United States to register with the government and reinstituted many of the prohibitions against political speech and action that had existed under the Espionage and Sedition acts in the late 1910s and early 1920s. The Smith Act was used to justify the suppression of a number of strikes in 1940 and early 1941, but when Germany broke its treaty and attacked the Soviet Union in 1941, the United States found itself suddenly allied with its erstwhile Communist foe. This alliance did not become firm until December 1941, when the

United States formally entered the war after the Japanese attack on Pearl Harbor. At that point, anti-Communist rhetoric and policy were suspended for most of the duration of the war. The influence of Dies and his incarnation of HUAC correspondingly waned and the committee was dissolved upon Dies's departure from Congress in 1944.

As the end of the war—and with it the end of the alliance of necessity with the Soviets—became more apparent in early 1945, Representative John E. Rankin (D-MS) quickly moved to reestablish HUAC, this time as a standing, or permanent, committee. By a 207–186 margin, the House approved the motion and within six months the groundwork was laid for HUAC's most spectacular investigation yet.

Investigating Hollywood

An initial attempt to seek out Communists in the motion picture industry in Hollywood had faltered in 1945, but once Representative J. Parnell Thomas (R-NJ) took over the chairmanship of the committee in 1947, he quickly rekindled the fire under this project. Emboldened by that year's passage of the Taft-Hartley Act, which forced all labor union leaders to sign a pledge disavowing communism, and armed with mountains of surveillance and background information produced (not always through legal means) by Hoover's FBI, Thomas opened hearings on October 20, 1947. The hearings began with a series of "friendly" witnesses who would testify that Communists were present but largely unwelcome in Hollywood. They were followed by a group of "unfriendly" witnesses who were suspected of inserting pro-Communist propaganda into Hollywood films. Historian Richard M. Fried claims that Thomas's division of witnesses in this manner speaks to his willingness to capitalize on infighting within Hollywood:

> In fact, Hollywood did serve as an oasis for the Communist Party, providing both the funds to grease Party causes and the glamour to grace them. . . . Some actors had flirted with communism, but the screenwriters, Hollywood's intelligentsia, were primarily the ones who joined the Party. . . . Hollywood also had a Right, which

nursed grievances against the Left and ascribed un-American views to it. . . . These conservatives shared the management view of the recent labor troubles [a series of crippling strikes among Hollywood studio workers in 1945 and 1946] and would provide the principal testimony against Hollywood's Left. Hollywood's divisions would be mirrored before HUAC.[2]

For days on end, studio executives and leading actors such as Ronald Reagan and Gary Cooper reassured the committee of the industry's patriotism, thereby setting themselves apart from the so-called "Hollywood Ten" who would follow. This group of eight screenwriters and two directors, all of whom were or had been members of the Communist Party, refused to cooperate with the committee's questioning and in some cases openly challenged its legality. Although they were initially supported in their protests by a group of leading Hollywood stars, including Humphrey Bogart and Frank Sinatra, the Hollywood Ten were punished severely for their refusal to cooperate. Not only were they professionally chastised when the heads of all the major studios "blacklisted" (refused to hire) them in November 1947, but they were all eventually imprisoned for terms of six months to a year for contempt of Congress.

Although the investigation itself had not produced much evidence of dire Communist infiltration, HUAC was nevertheless perceived as correct in its suspicions. Concurrently, the political divide between the United States and the Soviet Union—first called the "Cold War" by journalist Walter Lippmann in 1947—was widening and becoming more hostile. As a result, greater public attention (and anxiety) was devoted to its ongoing investigations into more sensitive areas, such as Soviet espionage in the nation's nuclear weapons program.

Nuclear Spies

After concluding its Hollywood probe HUAC turned its attention to nuclear espionage and quickly produced results. In August 1948 Elizabeth Bentley and Whittaker Chambers testified that they had participated in atomic spying and implicated several coconspirators. Among those implicated was a mid-level

State Department official named Alger Hiss, who appeared before HUAC two days after Chambers's testimony in an effort to clear his name. Representative Richard Nixon (R-CA) remained unimpressed by Hiss's explanations and for the next eighteen months he personally led the effort against Hiss. In doing so, Nixon helped make Hiss into the kind of polarizing symbol rarely seen since Sacco and Vanzetti. Despite a lengthy and intrusive FBI investigation, the evidence against Hiss did not support charges of espionage, so he was indicted on perjury charges resulting from conflicting statements he had made under oath about knowing Chambers personally. Hiss's first trial was inconclusive, but he was convicted on January 21, 1950, and would eventually serve nearly four years in prison.

As with the earlier Hollywood inquiry, the Hiss case hardly represented an overwhelming substantiation of the fears concerning Communist infiltration. Hiss was convicted on a legal technicality rather than tangible proof of spying, and the debate over his guilt or innocence continues to this day. Nevertheless, Nixon rode the celebrity of his efforts to the Senate in 1950, and HUAC gained further credibility due in large part to events outside the scope of the case. Barely two weeks after Hiss was convicted, a German-born British physicist named Klaus Fuchs, who had worked on the Manhattan Project, confessed to passing atomic secrets to the Soviets. Later that year Julius and Ethel Rosenberg were arrested on charges of atomic spying and their case captured the imagination of the entire nation over the next three years. The Soviets had successfully tested their first atomic bomb in August 1949, years ahead of most predictions, which convinced many Americans that the accused spies *must* be guilty. The establishment of the People's Republic of China in October 1949 and the outbreak of the Korean War in June 1950 furthered the fear that communism, now armed with nuclear weapons, was expanding its power rapidly and could soon destroy the United States.

The Rise and Fall of McCarthy

No one took more advantage of this fear than Joseph McCarthy. A largely undistinguished junior senator from Wisconsin prior to February 9, 1950, McCarthy burst upon the scene that day with a speech to the Women's Republican Club in Wheeling, West Virginia, in which he claimed to possess a list of names of Communists or Communist sympathizers serving in the State Department. Thriving on media attention he had never before received, McCarthy repeated these charges— though the number of alleged subversives varied from 205 to 57—in other speeches and again before the full Senate, until a subcommittee of the Senate Foreign Relations Committee was formed to look into his allegations. Chaired by Millard Tydings (D-MD), this subcommittee challenged McCarthy to produce his evidence, which he largely failed to do, and the committee ultimately concluded in July 1950 that McCarthy's charges were "a fraud and a hoax." The full Senate's vote on the committee's findings, however, fell along party lines, which allowed McCarthy to claim that Tydings was attempting to cover up the failings of his fellow Democrats—including President Harry S. Truman—in combating communism. McCarthy's comments were highlighted by the shocking victories by Communist forces during the early stages of the Korean War. As Fried notes: "As long as it lasted, the Korean War ensured the persistence of the politics of disloyalty on which McCarthy thrived." [3]

Despite his apparent scolding by the Tydings subcommittee, McCarthy actually emerged as a patriotic hero and rode that notoriety for the next four years.

HUAC and its Senate counterpart, the Senate Internal Security Subcommittee (SISS), continued to seek out Communist plots in all walks of American life. Hollywood was again singled out for scrutiny in 1951 as one of HUAC's fifty ongoing investigations. McCarthy was not yet a member of any formal committee at this point, which freed him to make a number of highly publicized speeches before anti-Communist groups. Meanwhile, SISS chairman Senator Pat McCarran (D-NV) expanded the scope of his Internal Security Act legislation of 1950 with the McCarran-Walter Act of 1952. By 1953 McCarthy's power became more institutionalized when he was appointed as chair of the Senate Permanent Subcommittee on Investigations. He quickly changed its mission from the mundane task of investigating inefficiency in government spending to a wide-ranging probe of Communist influence within the American government, especially the State Department. Together with fervent anti-Communists such as J.B. Matthews and Roy Cohn, McCarthy scoured the files of agency after agency looking for signs of "Red" infiltration.

In autumn 1953 McCarthy began to push his luck. The Korean War had ended after three bloody years in a stalemate and McCarthy decided to investigate whether this outcome stemmed from Communists working within the army. This implication outraged not only President Dwight D. Eisenhower, a former army general, but also veterans of both World War II and Korea. McCarthy's formal hearings were televised from April through June 1954, giving many Americans their first glimpse of "Tailgunner Joe" in action. McCarthy's tactics were succinctly condemned by army lawyer Joseph Welch on June 9, 1954, when he responded to one of McCarthy's attacks by asking "Have you no decency, sir, at long last?" The hearings ended with McCarthy in disgrace and the Senate voted to censure him in December 1954, effectively ending his influence. He died of liver failure in 1957 at the age of forty-nine, having lost his Senate reelection campaign the previous year.

Remnants of the Red Scare

Although McCarthy's precipitous fall from grace—coupled with the end of the Korean War—reduced the general tone of anti-Communist hysteria somewhat after 1954, it would be an overstatement to say that the second Red Scare ended completely with the demise of McCarthyism. HUAC's investigations of labor unions and the entertainment industry continued at a brisk pace throughout the 1950s, and it frequently delved into allegations of Communist ties among members of the civil rights and antiwar movements in the 1960s. It was renamed the Committee on Internal Security in 1969 and finally was abolished entirely in 1975.

Hoover also remained a highly visible crusader against communism after 1954, serving as FBI director until his death in 1972. Hoover launched the secret COINTELPRO (short for counterintelligence program) in 1956 with the intent of breaking up the CPUSA for good, a goal he had personally sought since his days as Palmer's deputy. In subsequent years COINTELPRO expanded its efforts to include white supremacists, labor unions, peace activists, feminists, environmentalists, and even Martin Luther King Jr., all of whom were associated in Hoover's mind with communism (and many of whom were concurrently investigated by HUAC). COINTELPRO's existence was revealed upon Hoover's death and immediately halted by his successor.

Even though opposition to communism remained a major political theme, especially after the fall of Cuba to Fidel Castro's pro-Soviet rebels in 1959, Fried notes that during the presidential election of 1960 "both candidates agreed that the danger flowed from Moscow, not some federal agency" and that "the domestic Communist issue hardly flickered in opinion polls."[4] As the government moved away from fanning the flames of anxiety about communism in the United States, that banner was taken up by independent groups like the Committee for the Present Danger, originally founded in 1950, and the John Birch Society, founded in 1958.

Nevertheless, the successful political career of former HUAC friendly witness Ronald Reagan suggests that antiradicalism was still as potentially powerful a strategy in 1980 as it had been for most of the previous hundred years.

Notes

1. Richard Hofstadter and Michael Wallace, eds., *American Violence: A Documentary History*. New York: Knopf, 1970, p. 19.
2. Richard M. Fried, *Nightmare in Red: The McCarthy Era in Perspective*. New York: Oxford University Press, 1990, pp. 74–75.
3. Fried, *Nightmare in Red*, p. 129.
4. Fried, *Nightmare in Red*, p. 194.

CHAPTER 1

Building Up the Red Scare

Communists Are Not Welcome in Hollywood

Ronald W. Reagan

At the time of his testimony before the House Committee on Un-American Activities (HUAC) on October 23, 1947, Ronald W. Reagan was among Hollywood's most prominent leading men and had starred in numerous successful films. Although Reagan's political career as governor of California and most famously as two-term Republican president of the United States did not begin until 1964, his conservative political views were evident in the testimony he offered before HUAC. Unlike the nineteen witnesses who were "blacklisted" (effectively banned from working in Hollywood) as suspected Communist sympathizers in the wake of HUAC's inquiries, Reagan was among a number of well-known film industry figures called to testify as "friendly witnesses" before the committee. When asked about the possible infiltration of Hollywood by Communists—a topic that consumed a substantial amount of the committee's efforts during the late 1940s—Reagan proved to be very accommodating. Although Reagan neither accused any of his fellow actors nor provided substantive evidence of widespread Communist activity in Hollywood, his status as president of the Screen Actors Guild—an influential organization of Hollywood actors—and his made-to-order answers to the committee's often loaded questions added considerable credence to the fear that "Reds" were trying to infiltrate the American motion-picture industry in order to spread communism and insert traitorous propaganda into films.

Ronald W. Reagan, testimony before the U.S. House Committee on Un-American Activities, Washington, DC, October 23, 1947.

The Committee met at 10:30 a.m., the Honorable J. Parnell Thomas (Chairman) presiding.

THE CHAIRMAN: The record will show that Mr. [John] Mc-Dowell (R-PA), Mr. [Richard] Vail (R-IL), Mr. [Richard] Nixon (R-CA), and Mr. Thomas are present. A Subcommittee is sitting. Staff members present: Mr. Robert E. Stripling, Chief Investigator; Messrs. Louis J. Russell, H.A. Smith, and Robert B. Gaston, Investigators; and Mr. Benjamin Mandel, Director of Research.

MR. STRIPLING: When and where were you born, Mr. Reagan?

MR. REAGAN: Tampico, Illinois, February 6, 1911.

MR. STRIPLING: What is your present occupation?

MR. REAGAN: Motion-picture actor.

MR. STRIPLING: How long have you been engaged in that profession?

MR. REAGAN: Since June 1937, with a brief interlude of three and a half years—that at the time didn't seem very brief.

MR. STRIPLING: What period was that?

MR. REAGAN: That was during the late war.

MR. STRIPLING: What branch of the service were you in?

MR. REAGAN: Well, sir, I had been for several years in the Reserve as an officer in the United States Cavalry, but I was assigned to the Air Corps.

MR. STRIPLING: That is kind of typical of the Army, isn't it?

MR. REAGAN: Yes, sir. The first thing the Air Corps did was loan me to the Signal Corps.

MR. MCDOWELL: You didn't wear spurs?

MR. REAGAN: I did for a short while.

THE CHAIRMAN: I think this has little to do with the facts we are seeking. Proceed.

MR. STRIPLING: Mr. Reagan, are you a member of any guild?

MR. REAGAN: Yes, sir, the Screen Actors Guild.

MR. STRIPLING: How long have you been a member?

MR. REAGAN: Since June 1937.

MR. STRIPLING: Are you the president of the guild at the present time?

MR. REAGAN: Yes, sir.

MR. STRIPLING: When were you elected?

MR. REAGAN: That was several months ago. I was elected to replace Mr. [Robert] Montgomery when he resigned.

MR. STRIPLING: When does your term expire?

MR. REAGAN: The elections come up next month.

MR. STRIPLING: Have you ever held any other position in the Screen Actors Guild?

MR. REAGAN: Yes, sir. Just prior to the war I was a member of the board of directors, and just after the war, prior to my being elected president, I was a member of the board of directors.

MR. STRIPLING: As a member of the board of directors, as president of the Screen Actors Guild, and as an active member, have you at any time observed or noted within the organization a clique of either Communists or Fascists who were attempting to exert influence or pressure on the guild?

MR. REAGAN: Well, sir, my testimony must be very similar to that of Mr. [George] Murphy and Mr. [Robert] Montgomery. There has been a small group within the Screen Actors Guild which has consistently opposed the policy of the guild board and officers of the guild, as evidenced by the vote on various issues. That small clique referred to has been suspected of more or less following the tactics that we associate with the Communist Party.

MR. STRIPLING: Would you refer to them as a disruptive influence within the guild?

MR. REAGAN: I would say that at times they have attempted to be a disruptive influence.

MR. STRIPLING: You have no knowledge yourself as to whether or not any of them are members of the Communist Party?

MR. REAGAN: No, sir, I have no investigative force, or anything, and I do not know.

MR. STRIPLING: Has it ever been reported to you that certain members of the guild were Communists?

MR. REAGAN: Yes, sir, I have heard different discussions and some of them tagged as Communists.

MR. STRIPLING: Would you say that this clique has attempted to dominate the guild?

MR. REAGAN: Well, sir, by attempting to put over their own particular views on various issues, I guess you would have to say that our side was attempting to dominate, too, because we were fighting just as hard to put over our views, and I think we were proven correct by the figures—Mr. Murphy gave the figures—and those figures were always approximately the same, an average of ninety per cent or better of the Screen Actors Guild voted in favor of those matters now guild policy.

Reagan Speculates About a Number of Organizations

MR. STRIPLING: Mr. Reagan, there has been testimony to the effect here that numerous Communist-front organizations have been set up in Hollywood. Have you ever been solicited to join any of those organizations or any organization which you considered to be a Communist-front organization?

MR. REAGAN: Well, sir, I have received literature from an organization called the Committee for a Far-Eastern Democratic Policy. I don't know whether it is Communist or not. I only know that I didn't like their views and as a result I didn't want to have anything to do with them.

MR. STRIPLING: Were you ever solicited to sponsor the Joint Anti-Fascist Refugee Committee?

MR. REAGAN: No, sir, I was never solicited to do that, but I found myself misled into being a sponsor on another occasion for a function that was held under the auspices of the Joint Anti-Fascist Refugee Committee.

MR. STRIPLING: Did you knowingly give your name as a sponsor?

MR. REAGAN: Not knowingly. Could I explain what that occasion was?

MR. STRIPLING: Yes, sir.

MR. REAGAN: I was called several weeks ago. There happened to be a financial drive on to raise money to build a badly needed hospital called the All Nations Hospital. I think the purpose of the building is so obvious by the title that it has the support of most of the people of Los Angeles. Certainly of most of the doctors. Some time ago I was called to the telephone. A woman introduced herself by name. I didn't make any particular note of her name, and I couldn't give it now. She told me that there would be a recital held at which [famed African American actor and singer] Paul Robeson would sing, and she said that all the money for the tickets would go to the hospital, and asked if she could use my name as one of the sponsors. I hesitated for a moment, because I don't think that Mr. Robeson's and my political views coincide at all, and then I thought I was being a little stupid because, I thought, Here is an occasion where Mr. Robeson is perhaps appearing as an artist, and certainly the object, raising money, is above any political consideration: it is a hospital supported by everyone. I have contributed money myself. So I felt a little bit as if I had been stuffy for a minute, and I said, "Certainly, you can use my name." I left town for a couple of weeks and, when I returned, I was handed a newspaper story that said that this recital was held at the Shrine Auditorium in Los Angeles under the auspices of the Joint Anti-Fascist Refugee Committee. The principal speaker was Emil Lustig [Ludwig?], Robert Burman took up a collection, and remnants of the Abraham Lincoln Brigade were paraded on the platform. I did not, in the newspaper story, see one word about the hospital. I called the newspaper and said I am not accustomed to writing to editors but would like to explain my position, and he laughed and said, "You needn't bother, you are about the fiftieth person that has called with the same idea, including most of the legitimate doctors who had also been listed as sponsors of that affair."

MR. STRIPLING: Would you say from your observation that that is typical of the tactics or strategy of the Communists, to solicit and use the names of prominent people to either raise money or gain support?

MR. REAGAN: I think it is in keeping with their tactics, yes, sir.

MR. STRIPLING: Do you think there is anything democratic about those tactics?

MR. REAGAN: I do not, sir.

MR. STRIPLING: As president of the Screen Actors Guild, you are familiar with the jurisdictional strike which has been going on in Hollywood for some time?

MR. REAGAN: Yes, sir.

MR. STRIPLING: Have you ever had any conferences with any of the labor officials regarding this strike?

MR. REAGAN: Yes, sir.

MR. STRIPLING: Do you know whether the Communists have participated in any way in this strike?

MR. REAGAN: Sir, the first time that this word "Communist" was ever injected into any of the meetings concerning the strike was at a meeting in Chicago with Mr. William Hutchinson, president of the carpenters' union, who were on strike at the time. He asked the Screen Actors Guild to submit terms to Mr. [Richard] Walsh, and he told us to tell Mr. Walsh that, if he would give in on these terms, he in turn would run this [Herbert K.] Sorrell and the other Commies out—I am quoting him—and break it up. I might add that Mr. Walsh and Mr. Sorrell were running the strike for Mr. Hutchinson in Hollywood.

Reagan Offers His Opinion on What to Do

MR. STRIPLING: Mr. Reagan, what is your feeling about what steps should be taken to rid the motion-picture industry of any Communist influences?

MR. REAGAN: Well, sir, ninety-nine per cent of us are pretty well aware of what is going on, and I think, within the bounds of our democratic rights and never once stepping over the rights given us by democracy, we have done a pretty good job in our business of keeping those people's activities curtailed. After all, we must recognize them at present as a political party. On that basis we have exposed their lies when we came across them, we have opposed their propaganda, and I can certainly testify that in the case of the Screen Actors Guild we have been eminently successful in preventing them from, with their usual tactics, trying to run a majority of an organization with a well-organized minority. In opposing those people, the best thing to do is make democracy work. In the Screen Actors Guild we make it work by insuring everyone a vote and by keeping everyone informed. I believe that, as Thomas Jefferson put it, if all the American people know all of the facts they will never make a mistake. Whether the Party should be outlawed, that is a matter for the Government to decide. As a citizen, I would hesitate to see any political party outlawed on the basis of its political ideology. We have spent a hundred and seventy years in this country on the basis that democracy is strong enough to stand up and fight against the inroads of any ideology. However, if it is proven that an organization is an agent of a foreign power, or in any way not a legitimate political party—and I think the Government is capable of proving that—then that is another matter. I happen to be very proud of the industry in which I work; I happen to be very proud of the way in which we conducted the fight. I do not believe the Communists have ever at any time been able to use the motion-picture screen as a sounding board for their philosophy or ideology. . . .

MR. CHAIRMAN: There is one thing that you said that interested me very much. That was the quotation from Jefferson. That is just why this Committee was created by the House of Representatives: to acquaint the American people with the facts. Once the American people are acquainted with the facts there is no question but what the American people will do the kind of a job that they want done: that is, to make America just as pure as we can possibly make it. We want to thank you very much for coming here today.

MR. REAGAN: Sir, I detest, I abhor their philosophy, but I detest more than that their tactics, which are those of the fifth column, and are dishonest, but at the same time I never as a citizen want to see our country become urged, by either fear or resentment of this group, that we ever compromise with any of our democratic principles through that fear or resentment. I still think that democracy can do it.

How I Helped Convict a Communist Agent

Whittaker Chambers

Whittaker Chambers was a struggling writer who had been associated with the Communist Party during the late 1930s. There is disagreement about the actual nature of his involvement: Chambers claimed he had been a Soviet spy for several years, but others disputed this claim as self-aggrandizement. He was subpoenaed to appear before the House Committee on Un-American Activities (HUAC) late in 1948, at which time he testified that he had received classified documents from a minor State Department official named Alger Hiss during the 1930s and that he had then passed these documents to Soviet spies. Because Chambers's testimony was somewhat contradictory and because of legal technicalities, Hiss could not be charged with espionage, but he was nevertheless accused of perjury—lying under oath in court—in responding to Chambers's testimony. Hiss's case seemed to validate fears that Communists were hiding out within the government. Several fervently anti-Communist politicians, notably a young California congressman named Richard Nixon, took it on themselves to convict Hiss, thereby creating the first major public spectacle of the Red Scare. Hiss's first trial in 1949 ended in a hung jury, but he was convicted in a second trial in 1950. Chambers discusses the process of gathering evidence and building the case for that second trial—a process that became as much political as legal—in this excerpt from his autobiography, which became a best-seller less than two years after Hiss's conviction. Hiss served nearly four years in prison, but maintained his innocence until his death in 1996.

Whittaker Chambers, *Witness*. New York: Random House, 1952. Copyright © 1952 by Whittaker Chambers. All rights reserved. Reproduced by permission of the publisher.

The years changed. 1948 passed into 1949. Among the years, 1949 is to me the dead year, a dreariness differentiated chiefly by spasms of a public pang. It opened with a new Grand Jury sitting in New York. It ended while for the second time a trial of Alger Hiss was dragging toward its close. It was the year in which I endured the ordeal of preparation and public testimony in the Hiss trial that was for me the probation, which must set the seal of integrity upon all my earlier acts.

In the first months of the new year, I continued my testimony before the new Grand Jury. I had already begun with the F.B.I. what amounted to a total recall of my life. It amassed all that I could remember about Communism and Communists in the United States and elsewhere. In report-form it made a fair-sized book.

Two special agents of the F.B.I., usually Tom Spencer and Frank Plant, worked with me on this project. We worked together for several months, from about ten o'clock in the morning until five o'clock in the evening, sending out for our lunch of coffee and sandwiches, which we ate at our desk. Merely the effort of such a total recollection is wearing. The recollection itself is exhausting. The great intelligence, tact and understanding with which Spencer and Plant brought me through that difficult experience, more than anything else, first moved my respect for the methods of the F.B.I. and won my trust on the human level.

Meanwhile, the immense investigation that preceded and accompanied the Hiss trials was going on. In time, there was probably no field office of the F.B.I. in the country that was not somehow engaged in that investigation. I could not fail to be impressed by the energy with which the organization as a whole, and the agents individually, threw themselves into their work. [Two previous witnesses, Henry J.] Wadleigh and [Vincent] Reno had early confirmed those parts of my story that concerned them. Other witnesses confirmed more. On the slim chance that my vague recollection of his real name might be right, the F.B.I. began to look for "Keith." In a few hours they had found him. To the Grand Jury and the F.B.I., that highly important witness corroborated my testimony, adding some facts that I had forgotten or never known.

Chambers Leads the F.B.I. Investigators

On the chance that I might be able to locate the former residence of the underground photographer, known only as "Felix," two F.B.I. agents and I sloshed one night around the snowy streets of Baltimore. As I have written earlier, I had glimpsed the apartment house where Felix had lived only once, for a few minutes, ten years or more before. I reconstructed as well as I could where I had then sat in a parked automobile, and sighting a block of apartments, said to the agents: "Try there." Within twelve hours, the F.B.I. had located Felix' old apartment, had discovered that his full name was Felix Inslerman, and had found him near Schenectady, N.Y.

There was a man with whom Hiss and someone else had attempted espionage dealings. I believed that the man was dead and said so. The F.B.I., checking back on my lead, found him alive. To the Grand Jury and the F.B.I., he confirmed my account of his dealings with Alger Hiss and others.

There were no "breaks" in the Hiss Case such as are common in more routine cases. The Communist conspiracy was too effective. The events involved had happened too long before. Time had effaced or changed too much. The far-flung investigation was a matter of daily grind varied by flashes of great probative intelligence. It is not my intention to discuss the details even of that part of it which I could observe. Much of it was beyond my sight. I will merely note that I myself was an object of its most intensive probing. Everything that I had said or done, every scrap of information I gave, every charge or rumor against me had to be laboriously checked and rechecked. In time, I came to feel that the F.B.I. knew much more about me than I knew about myself.

In time, too, the scores of agents whom I was constantly dealing with began to take form for me as human beings. I began to know about their gripes and special interests, their families, their troubles and their hopes. It is in those human terms that I mean to speak of the F.B.I. and its agents. For it is in those terms, which few ever think of, rather than its organizational expertness, which everybody knows about, that my memory of the F.B.I. is most personal and most grateful. It reached its pitch in the days of my testimony in the two Hiss trials.

In the morning before I went into court, at the lunch recess, in the evening, when I had finished testifying for the day and simply sat still for an hour or so to drain [Hiss's attorneys] Lloyd Paul Stryker or Claude Cross out of my system, the agents, singly, or in twos and threes, would come to sit with me. By their comments and conjectures on the progress of the fight, by gossip, by banter or a few considerate words quietly dropped—the immemorial, simple ways by which men have always kept up one another's morale in trouble, they kept up mine. They were like sturdier brothers in those days. I could catalogue their names. They would be meaningless to others. They know who they were and what they did, and why, when I hear that someone, like Max Loewenthal [author of a 1951 book critical of the F.B.I.], has been shaken by fears that the F.B.I. is a potentially dangerous secret police, I smile, suspecting that, in general, such fears measure the F.B.I.'s effectiveness in the nation's interest. For how can those men be dangerous to the nation who, as at present headed and organized, are, in fact, the nation itself, performing its self-protective function?

Chambers Claims to Be Persecuted by Communists

The tremendous investigation was paced by the tremendous public defamation of me. I do not believe that there is a scrap of real evidence to show that the Communist Party inspired and from time to time stepped up the voltage of that vilification. Those who insist plaintively on evidence against a force whose first concern is that there shall be no evidence against it, must draw what inferences they please. Few who know anything about Communists will doubt what cloaca [sewer] fed that bilge across the land.

It was avidly blotted up by much more articulate, widespread and socially formidable circles. In accusing Hiss of Communism, I had attacked an architect of the U.N., and the partisans of peace fell upon me like combat troops. I had attacked an intellectual and a "liberal." A whole generation felt itself to be on trial—with pretty good reason too, for its fears probably did not far outrun its guilt. From their roosts in the great cities, and certain collegiate eyries, the left-wing intellectuals of almost every feather (and that was most of the vocal intellectuals in the country) swooped and hovered in flocks like fluttered sea fowl—puffins, skimmers, skuas and boobies—and gave vent to hoarse cries and defilements. I had also accused a "certified gentleman," and the "conspiracy of the gentlemen" closed its retaliatory ranks against me. Hence that musk of snobbism that lay rank and discrepant over the pro-Hiss faction. Hence that morganatic bond between the forces of the left and the forces of the right (a director of a big steel company, the co-owner of a great department store, a figure high in the Republican organization, come quickly to mind) which made confusing common cause in exculpating Hiss by defaming Chambers.

There was another, less tangible bond between those circles which, together, accounted for a large part of the articulate American middle class. Both groups lived fairly constantly in the psychoanalyst's permanent shadow, and few articles of furniture were less dispensable to them than a couch. And they shared a common necessity. Since my charge against Alger Hiss was that he had been a Communist and a Soviet agent, and there was, besides the Grand Jury's perjury indictment, a good deal of clear and simple evidence that he had been, something, anything at all must be believed rather than the common-sense conclusion. The old masters—[Sigmund] Freud and the author [Austrian psychiatrist Richard von Krafft-Ebing] of the *Psychopathia Sexualis*—were conned again. No depravity was too bizarre to "explain" Chambers' motives for calling Hiss a Communist. No hypothesis was too preposterous, no speculation too fantastic, to "explain" how all those State Department documents came to be copied on Hiss's Woodstock typewriter. Only the truth became too preposterous to entertain. The great smear campaign was the real red herring in the Hiss Case.

Meanwhile, there sifted in on me warnings that the Hiss Case would never come to trial (repeated postponements made this seem all too probable), that the Government meant to throw the trial, that the Government's prosecutor would be fixed, and infinite variations. I crowded most of these warnings out of my mind, for a man has only so much strength, and I could not have gone on if I had given them active credence. Those that I could not quite ignore, I discounted. But even when I had discounted them to the limit of human mischief and imaginative folly, there still remained something that I could not discount. Neither could I be sure exactly what it was. Its contours became somewhat clearer in the antics of the first Hiss trial. But in the bleak spring of 1949, I did not believe that there was an outside chance for justice in the Hiss Case. It seemed to me that nothing short of a minor miracle could save the Hiss Case for the nation. And, in fact, something was in store that no action of my mind could have foreseen.

Chambers Recalls Thomas Murphy

One day, Tom Spencer broke into our routine talks to say that the Government's prosecutor for the Hiss trial had been chosen. "Who?" I asked quietly, for I knew that almost everything hinged on that choice. "Tom Murphy," said Tom Spencer. The name meant nothing to me. "Is it good?" I asked. "It is good," said Spencer.

I did not see Thomas F. Murphy until shortly before the first Hiss trial. He had scarcely undertaken the case before he had to undergo an operation. Once he came down to the farm, together with a trio of F.B.I. agents, to talk to my wife for the first time, and to discuss, among other things, the simple mechanics of a trial of which my wife and I knew almost nothing—where the jury sat, what the judge did, what the lawyers did. Later, I talked with Murphy briefly in the Federal Building. "Do you really believe that you can stand it," he asked me, "with all those people sitting there and the press writing down everything?" "I think you will find," I said, "that I am not in any way a coward." Murphy turned and stared sadly out of the window (he knew much more about trials than I did). "No," he said at last, "I don't believe you are." Among all the other doubts and pressures of that time, his words puzzled me and I left him in a deep depression.

During the first Hiss trial, Murphy and I had no direct communication. What I saw of him, I saw only in the seven days, more or less, when I was on the stand. The experience was too new to me, and I was kept too busy plucking harpoons out of my skin, to form any opinion about Murphy. In the whirling atmosphere of that courtroom, with Lloyd Paul Stryker spinning and flailing like a dervish, and Judge [Samuel] Kaufman snapping "Denied" to most of the Government motions, the last thing I took much thought of was the Government's prosecutor. But his summation to the jury impressed me greatly. More important, it seems to have impressed the jury.

Then, between the Hiss trials, Murphy visited the farm again. To me he seemed almost another man. His grasp of the intricacies of the Hiss Case was now firm and supple. He was at ease with it with the relaxed authority of a man who has mastered an art and now wants to practice it. He understood the Case, not only as a problem in law. He understood it in its fullest religious, moral, human and historical meaning. I saw that he had in him one of the rarest of human seeds—the faculty for growth, combined with a faculty almost as rare—a singular magnanimity of spirit. Into me, battered and gray of mood after a year of private struggle and public mauling, he infused new heart, not only because of what he was, but because he was the first man from the Government who said to me in effect: "I understand." I needed no more.

The whole nation now gratefully knows that six-foot-four, stalwart figure, with the mild but firm face, and the moustache. It knows what he has done. It watched him do it. I cannot add to that knowledge, except to point out this.

When Thomas Murphy decided, somewhat reluctantly, to take the Hiss Case, almost nobody had ever heard of him. Within the Justice Department he was known as a man who had never lost a case. Otherwise, he was a man who jostled no one, for he seemed without ambition beyond his immediate work. And he was so little caught in the enveloping atmosphere of politics that he was presently discovered not even to belong to a political club. Yet when the historic moment came, Murphy was waiting there at the one point in time and place where he could bring all that he was and all that life had made him to bear with decisive effect for the nation.

It is inconceivable to me that any other man could have replaced him. That is why I can think of his role only in this way: "It pleased God to have in readiness a man." . . .

Why Chambers Saw the Hiss Case as Important

No feature of the Hiss Case is more obvious, or more troubling as history, than the jagged fissure, which it did not so much open as reveal, between the plain men and women of the nation, and those who affected to act, think and speak for them. It was, not invariably, but in general, the "best people" who were for Alger Hiss and who were prepared to go to almost any length to protect and defend him. It was the enlightened and the powerful, the clamorous proponents of the open mind and the common man, who snapped their minds shut in a pro-Hiss psychosis, of a kind which, in an individual patient, means the simple failure of the ability to distinguish between reality and unreality, and, in a nation, is a warning of the end.

It was the great body of the nation, which, not invariably, but in general, kept open its mind in the Hiss Case, waiting for the returns to come in. It was they who suspected what forces disastrous to the nation were at work in the Hiss Case, and had suspected that they were at work long before there was a Hiss Case, while most of the forces of enlightenment were poohpoohing the Communist danger and calling every allusion to it a witch hunt. It was they who, when the battle was over, first caught its real meaning. It was they who almost unfailingly understood the nature of the witness that I was seeking to make, as I have tested beyond question whenever I have talked to any group of them. And it was they who, in the persons of the men I have cited, produced the forces that could win a struggle whose conspicuous feature is that it was almost without leadership. From the very outset, I was in touch with that enormous force, for which I was making the effort, and from which I drew strength. Often I lost touch with it or doubted it, cut off from it in the cities, or plunged in the depths of the struggle. But when I came back to it, it was always there. It reached me in letters and messages of encouragement and solicitude, understanding, stirring, sometimes wringing the heart. But even when they did not understand, my people were always about me. I had only to look around me to see them— on the farms, on the streets, in homes, in shops, in the day coaches of trains. My people, humble people, strong in common sense, in common goodness, in common forgiveness, because all felt bowed together under the common weight of life.

And at the very end of the Hiss Case, I heard their speaking voice, like themselves, anonymous, and speaking not to me as an individual, but to me in the name of all those who made the struggle.

The Threat of Communism Justifies Tough Tactics

Joseph McCarthy

Joseph McCarthy's name is arguably more closely associated with the Red Scare than any other name; it even became an "ism"—McCarthyism—encapsulating the political tactics of the anti-Communist movement of the 1940s and 1950s. In February 1950, McCarthy, a first-term Wisconsin Republican senator, traveled to Wheeling, West Virginia, where he gave a speech in which he unexpectedly made the shocking claim that there were hundreds of Communists working in the State Department and that he possessed a list of 205 of their names. Coming in the wake of the first Alger Hiss trial and the increasing visibility of hearings on similar subjects being held by the House Committee on Un-American Activities, McCarthy's claims quickly prompted an investigation headed by Senator Millard Tydings (D-MD). Tydings's committee dismissed McCarthy's charges as baseless, but McCarthy's reputation as a crusader against hidden Communists had been established nevertheless. In this excerpt from a book written in 1952, at the peak of his influence in Washington, McCarthy not only addresses the findings of the Tydings committee—with whose findings he naturally disagrees—but also defends his own methods. He claims that he is fighting for the survival of the country against a determined enemy and that such a fight justifies his tactics, especially given

Joseph McCarthy, "Round I—Wheeling, West Virginia," *McCarthyism: The Fight for America*. New York: Devin-Adair, 1952.

the unwillingness for such a fight that he perceives in other politicians. He singles out President Harry Truman and four Democratic senators running for president in 1952 for their lack of commitment in addressing the threat of communism.

During the public phase of my fight to expose pro-Communists and Communist treason in government, a vast number of deeply disturbed Americans have asked a multitude of questions. They want the answers—documented and proved—so they may determine for themselves the true situation.

This book is my answer to those questions. This is my answer to every American who seeks to know the truth about my fight against pro-Communists and Communist treason in government. As you read the carefully documented answers to the questions those Americans have asked over the past two years, I am confident you will agree that this fight is your fight—your fight for your children and your children's children. . . .

A Question of Methods and Results

I have often heard people say "I agree with Senator McCarthy's aim of removing Communists from government, but I do not agree with his methods." Senator, why don't you use methods which could receive the approval of everyone?

I have followed the method of publicly exposing the truth about men who, because of incompetence or treason, were betraying this nation. Another method would be to take the evidence to the President and ask him to discharge those who were serving the Communist cause. A third method would be to give the facts to the proper Senate committee which had the power to hire investigators and subpoena witnesses and records.

The second and third methods listed above were tried without success. The President [Harry S. Truman] apparently considered any attempt to expose Communists in the government as a cheap political trick to embarrass him and would not even answer a letter offering him evidence of Communist infiltration. The result of my attempt to give the evidence to a Senate committee (the Tydings Committee) is well known [Tydings's committee rejected McCarthy's charges of communists in the State Department in 1950]. Every person I named was white-washed and given a clean bill of health. The list included one who has since been convicted and others who have been discharged under the loyalty program.

The only method left to me was to present the truth to the American people. This I did. Even though the Administration has been fine-tooth combing my evidence for over 2 years, they have been unable to find a single item of that evidence that was untrue.

One of the safest and most popular sports engaged in today by every politician and office seeker is to "agree with McCarthy's aim of getting rid of Communists in government," but at the same time to "condemn his irresponsible charges and shot-gun technique." It is a completely safe position to take. The Communist Party and their camp followers in press and radio do not strike back as long as you merely condemn Communism in general terms. It is only when one adopts an effective method of digging out and exposing the under-cover, dangerous, "sacred cow" Communists that all of the venom and smear of the Party is loosed upon him.

I suggest to you, therefore, that when a politician mounts the speaker's rostrum and makes the statement that he "agrees with McCarthy's aims but not his methods," that you ask him what methods he himself has used against Communists. I suggest you ask him to name a single Communist or camp follower that he has forced out of the government by his methods.

I do not much mind the Communists screaming about my methods. That is their duty as Communists. They are under orders to do just that. But it makes me ill deep down inside when I hear cowardly politicians and self-proclaimed "liberals," too lazy to do their own thinking, parrot over and over this Communist Party line. By constant repetition they deceive good, loyal Americans into believing that there is some easy, delicate way of exposing Communists without at the same time exposing all of their traitorous, sordid acts.

Whenever I ask those who object to my methods to name the "objectionable methods," again I hear parroted back to me the Communist *Daily Worker* stock phrase "irresponsible charges" and "smearing innocent people." But as often as I have asked for the name of a single innocent person who has been "smeared" or "irresponsibly charged," nothing but silence answers.

When you hear a politician assuring you that "I am against Communism, but do not like McCarthy's methods," you might ask yourself this question: "Is this politician willing and eager to be against Communism on the speaker's stand but afraid to pay the high price in smear and abuse which is heaped upon anyone who really starts to draw blood from the Communist conspiracy?" During this fall's campaign, timid, cautious politicians who want to stay at the public trough regardless of the cost to the nation and those who would protect Communism and corruption in government will parrot over and over the same stock excuse. They will tell you how "vigorously" they "condemn" Communism. With equal vigor they will tell you that they condemn McCarthy for taking off his gloves and painfully digging out, one by one, the Administration-protected Communists.

The last 20 years have proved that even the most eloquent speeches against Communism *generally,* are as ineffective as speeches against crime *generally* by a prosecuting attorney who fails to dig out and convict the dangerous criminals.

When I launched the public phase of this fight at Wheeling, West Virginia, on February 9, 1950, I discussed, among others, the case of John Stewart Service. At the time I was discussing the Service case with the people at Wheeling, Service was in India. He had just arrived in that country. His task was to advise the State Department on a policy toward India. India was then facing a threat from Communism as serious as was China when Service represented the State Department there. I discussed point by point how John Service had contributed to the disastrous policy which sold 400 million Chinese to Communism. Had I merely discussed in general terms how disastrous our policy in China had been or how seriously India was threatened by Communism, Service obviously would not have been recalled, nor would he have been slowed down one iota in his planning.

For the last six years we have been losing the war against Communism at the rate of 100 million people a year. Anyone watching our civilization plunge so rapidly toward the abyss of oblivion, must conclude that we are losing the war to Communism for one of two reasons. We are losing either because of stumbling, fumbling idiocy on the part of those allegedly leading the fight against Communism or became, like Hiss, they are "planning it that way."

I have maintained that regardless of whether our defeat is because of treason or because of incompetence, those doing the planning should be removed from power if this nation and our civilization are to survive. My efforts have been in that direction and will continue to be so.

Alternative Approaches Have Not Been Suggested

Have those who have criticized your "methods" of fighting Communists demonstrated any other method of exposing treason?

In answering this question let us consider the most recent attack upon my "methods." On the date this manuscript goes to the printer, May 18, 1952, the press carries the story of four attacks upon "McCarthyism" and "McCarthy's methods." The attacks, according to the press, were made before the National Convention of the Americans for Democratic Action by four men who are asking the American people to place them at the helm of this government—candidates for President. The candidates were [Estes] Kefauver (D-TN), [Hubert] Humphrey (D-MN), [Director of Mutual Security Averill] Harriman, and [Brien] McMahon (D-CT). Each with apparently equal vigor condemned McCarthy's method of exposing Communists. All four of these men who ask to be elected President know that 10 of those whom I originally named before the Tydings Committee and who were cleared by that committee have since either been convicted or removed from the State Department under the loyalty program.

Therefore, the following questions should be asked those candidates for President:

(1) If elected President will you reinstate and return to positions of power those who were exposed and forced out of the State Department by McCarthy?

(2) Can you name one person whom you have exposed and had removed from government because he was either a Communist or a loyalty or security risk?

(3) Despite the opposition of the vast power of your party which had been in control of the federal government, Senator McCarthy has forced out of high position 10 of those whom he originally named. Three of you are on Senate Committees controlled by your party. You have the power to subpoena. You know the names of the Communist traitors as well as McCarthy does. There are still nearly six months before the November elections. This gives you time to prove that you can remove more Communists and loyalty and security risks by your method than McCarthy has removed by his. He has challenged you to do that. Will you accept that challenge?

(4) If with your combined efforts you are unable in the next six months to remove from government one Communist or loyalty or security risk as compared to McCarthy's record of 10, then are not the American people entitled to conclude that you are attacking McCarthy's fight against Communists because of either stupidity or dishonesty? . . .

Explaining an Apparent Inconsistency

Will you explain your use of the numbers 205 and 57 in your Wheeling speech?

At Wheeling I discussed a letter which Secretary of State [James] Byrnes wrote in 1946 to Congressman Adolph Sabath (D-IL). In that letter Byrnes stated that 284 individuals had been declared by the President's security officers as unfit to work in the State Department because of Communist activities and for other reasons, but that only 79 had been discharged. This left a balance of 205 who were still on the State Department's payroll even though the President's own security officers had declared them unfit for government service.

In the same speech at Wheeling, I said that while I did not have the names of the 205 referred to in the Byrnes letter, I did have the names of 57 who were either members of or loyal to the Communist Party. The following day I wired President Truman and suggested that he call in Secretary of State [Dean] Acheson and ask for the names of the 205 who were kept in the State Department despite the fact that Truman's own security officers had declared them unfit to serve. I urged him to have Acheson tell him how many of the 205 were still in the State Department and why. I told the President that I had the names of 57. I offered those names to the President. The offer was never accepted. The wire was never answered.

The Tydings Committee reported that you said you had the names of 205 and not merely the names of 57 when you spoke in Wheeling. What are the facts?

This question is best answered by Daniel Buckley, an investigator for the completely unfriendly Gillette-Monroney Committee which is investigating Senator [William] Benton's (D-CT) charge that I should be expelled from the Senate because of my fight against Communists. Buckley lost his job with the committee because of his efforts to get to the truth about the "numbers game." The committee sent him to Wheeling to get evidence on this question of the numbers used in my Wheeling speech. The affidavits which he obtained from a large number of witnesses confirmed my report of what was said.

In a public statement released to the press on December 27, 1951, Buckley said:

> My job in Wheeling, I thought was to find the facts, to find whether, as Senator Benton charged, Senator McCarthy had said that he had a list of 205 Communists in the State Department, or whether, as Senator McCarthy maintained, he had said he had a list of 57 individuals either members of or loyal to the Communist Party.

> While in Wheeling, I conscientiously interviewed a large number of witnesses who were in a position to know what Senator McCarthy had actually said. Every one of

these witnesses, save one, supplied information which cast grave doubt and suspicion on Senator Benton's story and substantially corroborated Senator McCarthy's account of the facts.

After conducting this investigation in Wheeling, Buckley stated that he returned to Washington and filed his report. He declared that Millard Tydings, who was no longer a member of the Senate, thereupon phoned him and questioned him about his findings.

When he advised Tydings that the witnesses had confirmed my statements about the use of the number 205 and 57, Buckley stated:

Senator Tydings became highly indignant and irritated. I soon found myself on my way back to Wheeling, this time accompanied by our chief investigator for the unusual purpose of double checking on my original report.

Buckley reported as follows on that second trip to Wheeling:

The information I developed on the second Wheeling trip did more than merely cast grave doubt and suspicion on Senator Benton's story. The newly unearthed evidence demolished Senator Benton's charge in all material respects and thoroughly proved Senator McCarthy's account of the facts to be truthful. . . .

McCarthy Denies a Political Motivation

Is this fight against Communists in government a fight against the Democrat Administration?

No, only against those in the Administration who have joined forces to protect Communists in government. If America is to win this battle, all loyal Democrats and Republicans must join forces against the Communist conspiracy.

Unfortunately, the Administration branch of the Democrat party feels that having coddled and protected Communists in government over the past years, it must now for political reasons avoid having them exposed. For the Administration to label the Democrat party as the protector of Communists is extremely unfair to the millions of Americans who have long voted the Democrat ticket. Certainly, those Democrats dislike Communists as much as the average Republican. All thinking Democrats and Republicans must admit that we are paying today—in lives in [the] Korea[n War] and in taxes from every week's payroll—because we completely failed to win the peace following World War II and that since then we have followed a foreign policy that is in the interest of international Communism, not America.

What a Communist America Would Look Like

J. Edgar Hoover

J. Edgar Hoover's career in law enforcement had an anti-Communist focus almost from the beginning. He took part in the so-called Palmer raids, in which suspected Communists were rounded up and deported during the first great Red Scare in 1919, and then quickly rose to the post of director of the Federal Bureau of Investigation (FBI) in 1924. He would serve eight different presidents in this job through 1972, overseeing the country's highest law-enforcement organization during the height of the Cold War. Hoover made no secret of his ardent opposition to Communism and devoted a sizable share of his agency's resources to assisting in the process of identifying and punishing Communists in all walks of American life. This excerpt from his best-selling 1958 book, *Masters of Deceit,* puts forth Hoover's vision of what would happen to the United States if Communists ever managed to seize power. Hoover argues not only that communism is an ideology completely contrary to American values but also that Americans should not drop their guard just because of temporary declines in the apparent number or influence of Communists in the country. The latter point is especially important since by the time of the book's publication, Joseph McCarthy had been forced to leave the Senate in disgrace, the House Committee on Un-American Activities'

J. Edgar Hoover, *Masters of Deceit: The Story of Communism in America and How to Fight It.* New York: Holt, Reinhart and Winston, 1958.

reputation had also been tarnished, and the public's focus on the issue had diminished. Hoover encourages vigilant awareness of the threat of communism and warns against naively thinking that "it can't happen here."

Many Americans have not stopped to realize what a "Soviet America" would mean. The communists, however, have no doubts. Their blueprints are already made. So, at the very outset, let us look at their dream and see what it would mean to you and me and all the people we know.

In June, 1957, Nikita Khrushchev, Soviet Communist Party boss, was interviewed before a nation-wide American television audience. With calm assurance he stated:

> . . . I can prophesy that your grandchildren in America will live under socialism. And please do not be afraid of that. Your grandchildren will . . . not understand how their grandparents did not understand the progressive nature of a socialist society.

William Z. Foster, former National Chairman of the Communist Party of the United States (now [1958] Chairman Emeritus of the Party's National Committee), also predicted that this nation will one day become communist when he stated in 1949, in dedicating his book, *The Twilight of World Capitalism:*

> To My Great-Grandson Joseph Manley Kolko Who Will Live in a Communist United States.

These words of Russia's top Party boss and one of the highest-ranking communists in the United States reveal the nature of the enemy we face. To make the United States a communist nation is the ambition of every Party member, regardless of position or rank. He works constantly to make this dream a reality, to steal your rights, liberties, and property. Even though he lives in the United States, he is a supporter of a foreign power, espousing an alien line of thought. He is a conspirator against his country.

The communist is thinking in terms of *now* [1958], in your lifetime. Remember that within four decades communism, as a state power, has spread through roughly 40 per cent of the world's population and 25 per cent of the earth's surface. Some years ago communists were complaining that their "fatherland," Soviet Russia, was encircled, a communist island in a "capitalist" sea. Today [in 1958] the situation is changed. The world communist movement is on the march, into Germany, the Balkans, the Middle East, stretching across the plains of Asia into China, Korea, and Indochina. Communists have never won over an entire country by a free election and have never hesitated to shed blood if this would best serve their purposes. Moreover, in noncommunist countries thousands of Party members are working for Moscow. Communists firmly believe they are destined to conquer the world.

This belief is held in the United States too. A disciplined Party of hard-core fanatical members is now at work, with their fellow travelers, sympathizers, opportunists, and dupes. Communists in our country, though small in numbers, do not feel lonely. They have faith in the "big Red brother" who will come to their help. William Z. Foster's hope, a Red America, is today inspiring thousands of Party members and sympathizers to determined effort. They want to add America to Soviet Russia's list of conquests.

Why Declining Membership Is Not a Sign of Weakness

In recent years there has been a tendency to discount the menace of domestic communists solely because of a decline in Party membership. In fact, some have gone so far as to say, " . . . the party . . . is almost over." Let's examine that statement:

In 1922, when Communist Party membership reached 12,400, William Z. Foster said, " . . . we no longer measure the importance of revolutionary organizations by size. In some places where there are only one or two men, more results are obtained than where they have larger organizations. . . ."

This has been the communist line down through the years. Foster in 1951 stated, "Communist strength . . . cannot be measured even approximately by statistics. . . . The Communist parties' strength runs far beyond all formal measurements. . . ."

The Party's membership in this country reached a low in 1930 when it had 7,500 members, and a peak of 80,000 in 1944; its membership at five-year intervals since 1930 has been as follows: 1935—30,000; 1940—55,000 (a drop of 15,000 from 1939); 1945—64,600 (a drop of 15,400 from 1944); 1950—43,200; 1955—22,600; and by the summer of 1957 membership had further declined. However, over the years it has been estimated by the communist leaders themselves that for every Party member ten others are ready, willing, and able to do the Party's work.

Fluctuations in the American Party parallel those in foreign countries. The record clearly establishes that Communist Parties have the power of swift and solid growth when the opportunity arises. The following figures reflect how Party membership can dwindle and then spurt:

In Italy, Party membership went from 6,000 in 1943 to 2,500,000 in 1951; in France, from 20,000 in 1929 to 400,000 in 1956; in Syria, from 250 in 1931 to 10,000 in 1956; in Brazil, from 25,000 in late 1947 to 100,000 in 1956; and in Indonesia, from 30,000 in 1953 to 500,000 in 1956. . . .

A Vision of Communist America

Under communism, a tiny minority, perhaps ten to twenty men, would rule the United States. An open dictatorship called the "dictatorship of the proletariat" would be established. Communists, in all their teachings, make this point clear. The capital city, as one communist leader pointed out, would be moved from Washington, D.C., to a large industrial center, probably Chicago. National as well as state and local governments would be eliminated. "Soviets" (meaning councils) would be formed throughout the nation. These would consist of local Communist Party henchmen who would depose and probably liquidate your mayor, chief of police, clergymen, and leading citizens.

The Constitution, and all our laws, would be abolished. If you owned productive property you would be arrested as an "exploiter," hauled before a revolutionary court, and sentenced to a concentration camp—that is, if you convinced the "judge" you were worth saving at all. All property used in production would be confiscated, thus leading ultimately to total communization, meaning state ownership. This confiscation would include your home, business, bank deposits, and related personal possessions. These would "belong to everybody." You have no "right" to own them under the communist scheme.

The revolution would affect every man, woman, and child in America. Communists do not propose to remodel our government or retain any part of it. They would tear it to the ground, destroy all opposition, and then create a new government, an American province in the Soviet world empire. Their recipe for action? The 1917 Soviet revolution, tailored to modern conditions. The communists themselves have made the claim:

> The principles upon which a Soviet America would be organized would be the same, in every respect, as those which guided the Soviet Union.

William Foster, long-time head of the communist movement in our country, has boasted that the communist revolution, after the actual seizure of power, would "develop even more swiftly" than the Russian.

All industry would be nationalized and farms taken away from their owners. A small businessman is just as guilty as a large businessman; both must be liquidated. Rents, profits, and insurance would be abolished. Countless occupations, termed by the communists as "useless and parasitic," would be ended. Here is a part of their list: wholesalers, jobbers, real estate men and stockbrokers, advertising specialists, traveling salesmen, lawyers, "whole rafts of government bureaucrats, police, clericals, and sundry capitalist quacks, fakers, and grafters." The communists have a special disdain for lawyers. Perhaps it is because there will be no need for lawyers when there are no rights to defend. At any rate, Foster has said, "The pest of lawyers will be abolished."

Action would be drastic, immediate, and without appeal. An armed "Red Guard" would enforce the orders of Party henchmen. Hotels, clubs, and swimming pools would be used for the benefit of "workers," meaning, in most cases, Party bosses. The workingman in the mines, factories, and mills would be told to work certain hours for certain wages. Labor unions, as we know them, would be obliterated. All such organizations would be owned and operated by the communist government, and no laborer would be permitted to organize a union or to strike against his "government."

The press would be muzzled, free speech forbidden, and complete conformity demanded. If you expressed an opinion contrary to the Party line, you should have known better and your "disappearance" would serve as a lesson for others. Fear becomes an enforcement technique. Movies, radio, and television would be taken over by the government as agencies for government propaganda. Churches would probably not be closed immediately, but they would be heavily taxed, their property seized by the state, and religious schools liquidated. Clergymen would be required to accept the Party line. "God does not exist. Why worship Him?" say the communists. Children would be placed in nurseries and special indoctrination schools. Women, boast the communists, would be relieved of housework. How? Huge factory and apartment-house kitchens would be set up, so that women would be "free" to work in factories and mines along with the men.

This picture of a communist America is not overdrawn. Here are the words of William Z. Foster:

> Under the dictatorship all the capitalist parties—Republican, Democratic, Progressive, Socialist, etc.—will be liquidated, the Communist party functioning alone as the Party of the toiling masses. Likewise, will be dissolved all other organizations that are political props of the bourgeois rule, including chambers of commerce, employers' associations, rotary clubs, American Legion, Y.M.C.A. and such fraternal orders as the Masons, Odd Fellows, Elks, Knights of Columbus, etc.

Under this schedule many Americans are eligible for liquidation not once but several times, depending on their present freely chosen affiliations and social interests.

Communism Is a Real Threat

Communism is many things: an economic system, a philosophy, a political creed, a psychological conditioning, an educational indoctrination, a directed way of life. Communists want to control everything: where you live, where you work, what you are paid, what you think, what streetcars you ride (or whether you walk), how your children are educated, what you may not and must read and write. The most minute details, even the time your alarm clock goes off in the morning or the amount of cream in your coffee, are subjects for state supervision. They want to make a "communist man," a mechanical puppet, whom they can train to do as the Party desires. This is the ultimate, and tragic, aim of communism.

These statements are confirmed, day after day, by documented reports from areas where communists have already taken over: Hungary, East Germany, Bulgaria, Poland, Roumania, Czechoslovakia, Red China, and other areas.

When you read such reports, do not think of them as something happening in a far-off land. Remember, always, that "it could happen here" and that there are thousands of people *in this country* now working in secret to make it happen here. But also, thank God, there are millions of Americans who oppose them. If we open our eyes, inform ourselves, and work together, we can keep our country free.

Communism Can and Must Be Fought at Home

John A. Stormer

John A. Stormer was a journalist and lecturer who became a vigorous anti-Communist activist in the late 1950s. Although Stormer's 1964 book *None Dare Call It Treason* appeared after the peak of the Red Scare, it clearly shows how the ideas propagated by the likes of Senator Joseph McCarthy and FBI director J. Edgar Hoover continued to influence Americans into the 1960s. Stormer gives his readers detailed advice about what they can do to combat the continuing menace of communism, the seriousness of which was reinforced during the Cuban Missile Crisis in October 1962. Stormer argues that successful anticommunism must be a blend of patriotism, education, organization, directed action, political engagement, and Christian commitment. In this regard, Stormer echoes the ideas of groups such as the John Birch Society, which became one of the foremost refuges for anti-Communists after the decline of McCarthyism and the onset of détente—a French term meaning peaceful coexistence—between the United States and the Soviet Union in the early 1970s.

D o we face a hopeless battle? Has time run out for America? The answer is up to *you.*

The end will not come when the commissars [i.e., Soviet leaders] finally haul 60-million hopelessly diseased, capitalistic

John A. Stormer, *None Dare Call It Treason.* Florissant, MO: Liberty Bell Press, 1964. Copyright © 1964 by John A. Stormer. All rights reserved. Reproduced by permission.

"animals" off to liquidation centers or when Communist Party Chief, Gus Hall, gets his wish to see the "last Congressman strangled to death with the guts of the last preacher."

If the battle is lost, the real end will come long before. It will come when those who oppose collectivism have been so discredited by smears, discouraged by disasters, or divided by dissenters that they can no longer continue to fight.

The end will come when businessmen accept "You can't fight city hall" as their philosophy and settle down to "exist" within the framework of a completely-controlled, federally-dominated economy. When fear of a lost government contract, an income tax audit, or the disfavor of a vocal customer is more important for most Americans than standing up for principle, the fight will be over.

The battle will be lost, not when freedom of speech is finally taken away, but when Americans become so "adjusted" or "conditioned" to "getting along with the group" that when they finally see the threat, they say, "I can't afford to be controversial." Time will run out for free men, when individuals read facts like those in this book, shrug their shoulders, and say, "What can one person do? It's too big to fight."

How far down that path are we? Look around and see for yourself. We are losing rapidly. A cold analysis of the world situation and of the degree of control exercised by the collectivists can only produce the realization that the odds against our survival are great.

The communists are extremely close to total victory. But it is not inevitable. Their one fear is that Americans will awake in time to the danger and do something about it.

That is our hope and our challenge.

What should you do?

Before his death, the late Congressman Francis Walter (D-Pa), who served for eight years as Chairman of the House Committee on Un-American Activities, gave Americans a brief, but concise, guide to follow. His statement, *How to Fight Communism,* said:

Get the facts . . . get the help of others . . . organize . . . act.

Building Up the Red Scare 55

The words of J. Edgar Hoover . . . tell how to get the facts. Mr. Hoover said of communism and its threat:

> The way to fight it is to study it, understand it, and discover what can be done about it. This cannot be accomplished by dawdling at the spring of knowledge; it can only be achieved by dipping deeply into thoughtful, reliable, and authoritative sources of information.

Two years earlier [in 1959], Mr. Hoover issued a similar statement, and added:

> This program must encompass, not only a penetrating study of Communism, but also a thorough grounding in the basic principles of our individual freedom under law.

Within those two statements can be found the basic guidelines for intelligent action against communism. Congressman Walter gave more detailed advice, saying:

> Get the facts. Study communism. You can't fight an enemy you don't know. This is a fundamental rule of warfare. Learn communism's basic doctrines, its strategy, its tactics; its line on current national and international affairs; the names of major communist fronts and leading communists and fellow travellers. This is minimum knowledge required for effective anti-communism.

Education and Organization Are Necessary Steps

Once you have informed yourself, the next most important job is awakening others. Congressman Walter gave this advice:

> Get the help of others. Two heads are better than one— and ten men are more powerful than two.

Before you can convince others you must gain their attention and build respect for your knowledge. The communists recognize this fact. In the official communist *Manual on Organization,* party members are given these instructions:

In order to win the confidence of the workers, the unit must be able to give a correct answer to every question which bothers the workers. The units must follow very carefully every step that is taken by the capitalist class in the city and county councils, state legislatures, and Congress and expose all their moves.

Can you do less? Communists use "facts" slanted to tell the communist story. They present them in person or in the propaganda they spread through the communications media they control. You can only combat the false propaganda with the truth.

To stay informed, once you get a basic knowledge, try to read at least two daily newspapers with opposite editorial viewpoints. In addition, subscribe to at least one weekly newspaper or magazine which specializes in depth coverage of conservative activities. . . .

Taking Action to Oppose Communism

Once you are informed—and have started to inform others—you must start acting. Knowledge without action produces demoralization. Congressman Walter gave this admonition:

> Knowledge that is not put to use is wasted. No matter how much you learn about communism, you will contribute nothing to the fight against it unless you . . . translate your learning into deeds that weaken communism.

Uncoordinated action has little effect. Too many concerned people jump from project to project, never completing any. Congressman Walter warned:

> Organize your helpers and plan your action. Mere numbers are not enough. Any project you undertake should have at least as much planning and organization as the communists normally put into their schemes. And that's plenty.

It is not necessary to form your own organization. Thousands have already been formed by concerned Americans, including this author. Many have been ineffective because of lack of resources, inability of part-time leadership to plan and supervise activities, and lack of coordinated effort between small groups.

There are a number of well established national organizations. Some, like the American Legion and the Daughters of the American Revolution oppose communism as part of their overall program. Others, like the John Birch Society, are primarily anti-communist organizations. Still others are formed for a single purpose, such as opposing Red China's admission to the UN. . . .

Concerned Americans should carefully investigate the goals, programs, policy, personnel, and leadership of these or other anti-communism organizations to decide for themselves how effective they are. Rather than judge solely on word of mouth or the sometimes slanted newspaper accounts, write to any or all for their literature.

Political Engagement Is Key

A program for victory over communism cannot be achieved until Americans elect a President and a Congress with the will to win *and* the courage to "cleanse" the policy-making agencies of government of those who, for one reason or another, have aided the communists down through the years. To accomplish this, conservative Americans must make their voices heard in the political parties.

The Communist Party General Secretary, Gus Hall, sees this danger to communism and is working to prevent it. In June 1963 he ordered communists to join with the "non-communist left" within the Democratic Party to elect candidates of the "people's political movements" (i.e., Red favored movements) and to . . .

> . . . single out for defeat such individuals as [Senator Kenneth] Keating [D-NY] and [Senator Thomas] Dodd [D-CT], as well as a number of others.

Hall specifically called for the purging from the Republican Party of the ultra-right (anti-communist) forces. Hall admitted that while "moderates" of the Eisenhower-Kuechel wing of the Republican Party had not lost out completely . . .

> as can be seen from the speech of Senator [Thomas] Kuechel of California . . . the alliance of the ultra-right and Conservative aggressive imperialist elements has pushed the Republican Party to the right.

Within two weeks after Hall's demand for defeat of the ultra-right in the Republican Party, a massive smear campaign was launched in major news media, with a lengthy article, *Rampant Right Invades the GOP,* in *Look* magazine's July 16, 1963 issue. [New York governor] Nelson Rockefeller called upon Senator Barry Goldwater to repudiate his ultra-right support. Drew Pearson and other prominent columnists, wittingly or unwittingly fell into line with the Gus Hall directive. Pearson accused Young Republicans of "fascist tactics" in electing a Goldwater supporter as their national chairman.

Within six weeks after Gus Hall issued his order against the ultra-right, the "purge" reached all the way down to the local level as "modern Republican" officials fired conservative precinct captains and workers.

Whether the American people, in general, and rank-and-file Republicans, in particular, will fall for the communist-led attack to drive the anti-communists out of key positions in the Republican Party will probably be a major factor in determining whether the battle against communism is won or lost. If the communists and the "liberal internationalists" control the presidential nominations in both parties in 1964, as they have for 30 years, the hope for victory over communism will receive a massive setback. Work in the party organizations by informed conservatives can prevent this.

Cries of "We are being sold out to the communists" or decrying the strength and success of the AFL-CIO [a major labor organization] machine will not win the 1964 elections. COPE [the AFL-CIO's lobbying organization] has devised no secret formula for winning elections. It puts into practice the instructions an obscure county chairman of the Whig Party gave his workers in 1840. His name was Abraham Lincoln, and he said:

. . . the following is the plan of organization . . . divide (your) county into small districts, and . . . appoint in each a subcommittee, whose duty it shall be to make a perfect list of all the voters in their respective districts, and to ascertain with certainty for whom they will vote . . . keep a constant watch on the doubtful voters, and from time to time have them talked to by those in whom they shall have the most confidence . . . on election days see that every Whig is brought to the polls.

Lincoln knew that elections are not necessarily won by the party or candidate which is right—but by the organization which gets its voters to the polls. Issues and beliefs of a candidate are important—but they cannot win unless they are backed by a functioning organization geared to locate friendly voters, register them, and get them to the polls on election day . . . then, keep the election honest.

Issues, properly used, can motivate average, apathetic citizens to become doorbell ringers for candidates with principles. Several thousand informed, motivated workers in a congressional district of several hundred thousand voters can turn the tide, *if they are properly trained, organized and directed.*

In 1962, for example, 29-year-old William Brock of Lookout Mountain, Tennessee ran for Congress in a district where Democrats outnumbered Republicans 8 to 1. Brock was a Republican, yet he was elected to Congress because his presentation of the issues attracted workers who put Lincoln's plan into action.

Half of the American people cannot be educated about communism overnight. However, if one out of every hundred citizens is alerted, educated and mobilized into a functioning political organization, they can nominate and elect good Americans in 1964.

The Religious Dimension of Anti-Communism

Conservatives can win the political battles necessary to insure America's survival—and still lose the long term war against communism.

J. Edgar Hoover gave the ultimate answer in accepting an award from the Freedom Foundation at Valley Forge on February 22, 1962. He said:

The basic answer to communism is moral. The fight is economic, social, psychological, diplomatic, strategic—but above all it is spiritual.

Another anonymous writer said the same thing in a slightly different way. His advice:

Pray to God with the knowledge that everything depends on him—and work as if everything depended on you.

Without God, man can accomplish nothing. Yet, today, unfortunately, millions of Americans attend churches which are "man-centered" rather than "God-centered." Millions of persons who call themselves Christians attend church regularly and have never heard the Bible message of personal and individual salvation.

The answer to man's problems, the solution to the peril facing America is found in the Holy Scriptures. In II Chronicles 7:14, God tells us:

If my people, which are called by my name, shall humble themselves and pray and seek my face, and turn from their wicked ways; then will I hear from heaven, and will forgive their sin, and will heal their land.

Communism Is a Grave Threat

There is much to be done if America is to block communist domination of the world. Much of the work is up to *you*.

First, you must educate yourself. Determine that the facts in this book are true. Then, alert and educate others. Stay informed—and start to act. Join with others who are already well-organized for the battle against communism.

Recognize that those who refuse to work politically to protect their freedom may someday face a choice between fighting with guns or becoming slaves. Avoid being sidetracked into ineffective, defensive actions. Most of all, avoid demoralization.

Examine your own personal religious beliefs. Is God a meaningful, consuming force in your life?

The books, literature and other aids you'll need all cost money. Political activity, even on the precinct level, involves expenses. Political campaigns, anti-communist organizations all need financial support. As you evaluate costs, remember that if rampant inflation comes to America your savings will be worthless. If Communism comes to America you will lose not only your money, but your freedom, your children, your home, and possibly your life.

The costs cannot be measured in money alone. Educating and alerting others will not make you popular. Many dedicated Americans have already suffered smears, economic sanctions, and personal attacks for standing up for what they knew was right. J. Edgar Hoover commented on this tragic fact in a speech to the Daughters of the American Revolution in 1954. Mr. Hoover said:

> In taking a stand for preservation of the American way of life, your organization became the target of vile and vicious attacks. So have all other patriotic organizations and, for that matter, every other person who has dared to raise his voice against communism. It is an established fact that whenever one has dared to expose the communist threat he has invited upon himself the adroit and skilled talents of experts of character assassination. The Federal Bureau of Investigation has stood year after year as taunts, insults and destructive criticism have been thrown its way.

> To me, one of the most unbelievable and unexplainable phenomena in the fight on Communism is the manner in which otherwise respectable, seemingly intelligent persons, perhaps unknowingly, aid the Communist cause more effectively than the Communists themselves. The pseudo liberal can be more destructive than the known communist because of the esteem which his cloak of respectability invites.

Six years later [in 1960], Mr. Hoover repeated much the same message, when in a letter to law enforcement officials, he said:

It is indeed appalling that some members of our society continue to deplore and criticize those who stress the communist danger. What these "misguided" authorities fail to realize is that the Communist Party, USA, is an integral part of international communism. As the world-wide menace becomes more powerful, the various Communist parties assume a more dangerous and sinister role in the countries in which they are entrenched. Public indifference to this threat is tantamount to national suicide.

Lethargy leads only to disaster. . . . Only the intelligent efforts of all Americans can prevent the decay of public apathy from laying open our Nation to the Red Menace.

Because the repeated warnings of J. Edgar Hoover and other great Americans have been suppressed, ignored, and ridiculed, only great sacrifices in time, energy and money will turn the tide.

The choice is yours. You can throw out your chest with pride and say, "It can't happen here." But nearly every one of the 800-million people captured by the communists since 1945 doubtless said the same thing.

The alternative is to begin immediately to educate yourself; to embark on a program of action. If you delay, your motivation will pass, your concern will recede, but the danger will increase.

The choice you must make was enunciated by Winston Churchill when he told the people of England:

If you will not fight for right when you can easily win without bloodshed; if you will not fight when your victory will be sure and not too costly; you may come to the moment when you will have to fight with all the odds against you and only a precarious chance of survival.

Because we have ignored warning after warning, we are now at that place in history. Unless you do your part now, you will face a further choice, also described by Mr. Churchill. He said:

> There may be even a worse case. You may have to fight when there is no hope of victory, because it is better to perish than live as slaves.

What will you do?

CHAPTER 2

Speaking Out Against the Red Scare

HUAC Is Abusing Its Power

John Howard Lawson

John Howard Lawson was a prominent Hollywood screenwriter with dozens of celebrated films to his credit when he was subpoenaed to appear before the House Committee on Un-American Activities (HUAC) on October 27, 1947. At the time, the committee was investigating the supposed infiltration of the Hollywood motion picture industry by Communists, with a particular focus on writers who might have been putting subversive messages into their scripts. Lawson was one of ten scheduled witnesses—including other well-known screenwriters such as Dalton Trumbo, Ring Lardner, and Alvah Bessie—who refused to answer the committee's questions. Most of these so-called unfriendly witnesses presented themselves before the committee but invoked their Fifth Amendment rights in an effort to publicly demonstrate their principled opposition to HUAC's tactics. In this transcript of Lawson's testimony, he not only objects to being asked leading questions but also states that the committee practices a double standard, treating witnesses making accusations of Communist associations differently from those being accused. Lawson and the rest of the so-called Hollywood Ten were blacklisted, effectively barred from working in Hollywood, for several decades as a consequence of their refusal to testify.

John Howard Lawson, testimony before the U.S. House Committee on Un-American Activities, Washington, DC, October 27, 1947.

The Committee met at 10:30 a.m., the Honorable J. Parnell Thomas (Chairman) presiding.

Staff members present: Mr. Robert E. Stripling, Chief Investigator; Messrs. Louis J. Russell, H. A. Smith, and Robert B. Gaston, Investigators; and Mr. Benjamin Mandel, Director of Research.

THE CHAIRMAN: The record will show that a Subcommittee is present, consisting of Mr. [Richard] Vail (R-IL), Mr. [John] McDowell (R-PA), and Mr. Thomas.

MR. LAWSON: Mr. Chairman, I have a statement here which I wish to make—

THE CHAIRMAN: Well, all right, let me see your statement. (*Statement handed to the Chairman.*)

THE CHAIRMAN: I don't care to read any more of the statement. The statement will not be read. I read the first line.

MR. LAWSON: You have spent one week vilifying me before the American public—

THE CHAIRMAN: Just a minute—

MR. LAWSON:—and you refuse to allow me to make a statement on my rights as an American citizen.

THE CHAIRMAN: I refuse to let you make the statement because of the first sentence. That statement is not pertinent to the inquiry. Now, this is a Congressional Committee set up by law. We must have orderly procedure, and we are going to have orderly procedure. Mr. Stripling, identify the witness.

MR. LAWSON: The rights of American citizens are important in this room here, and I intend to stand up for those rights, Congressman Thomas.

MR. STRIPLING: Mr. Lawson, will you state your full name, please?

MR. LAWSON: I wish to protest against the unwillingness of this Committee to read a statement, when you permitted [two previous witnesses, Hollywood producers] Mr. [Jack L.] Warner, Mr. [Louis B.] Mayer, and others to read statements in this room. My name is John Howard Lawson.

MR. STRIPLING: When and where were you born?

MR. LAWSON: New York City.

MR. STRIPLING: What year?

MR. LAWSON: 1894.

MR. STRIPLING: Give us the exact date.

MR. LAWSON: September 25.

MR. STRIPLING: Mr. Lawson, you are here in response to a subpoena which was served upon you on September 19, 1947; is that true?

MR. LAWSON: That is correct.

MR. STRIPLING: What is your occupation, Mr. Lawson?

MR. LAWSON: I am a writer.

MR. STRIPLING: How long have you been a writer?

MR. LAWSON: All my life—at least thirty-five years—my adult life.

Lawson Refuses to Answer the Committee

MR. STRIPLING: Are you a member of the Screen Writers Guild?

MR. LAWSON: The raising of any question here in regard to membership, political beliefs, or affiliation—

MR. STRIPLING: Mr. Chairman—

MR. LAWSON:—is absolutely beyond the powers of this Committee.

MR. STRIPLING: Mr. Chairman—

MR. LAWSON: But—

(*The Chairman pounding gavel.*)

MR. LAWSON: It is a matter of public record that I am a member of the Screen Writers Guild.

MR. STRIPLING: I ask—

(*Applause.*)

THE CHAIRMAN: I want to caution the people in the audience: You are the guests of this Committee and you will have to maintain order at all times. I do not care for any applause or any demonstrations of one kind or another.

MR. STRIPLING: Now, Mr. Chairman, I am also going to request that you instruct the witness to be responsive to the questions.

THE CHAIRMAN: I think the witness will be more responsive to the questions.

MR. LAWSON: Mr. Chairman, you permitted—

THE CHAIRMAN (*pounding gavel*): Never mind—

MR. LAWSON:—witnesses in this room to make answers of three or four or five hundred words to questions here.

THE CHAIRMAN: Mr. Lawson, you will please be responsive to these questions and not continue to try to disrupt these hearings.

MR. LAWSON: I am not on trial here, Mr. Chairman. This Committee is on trial here before the American people. Let us get that straight.

THE CHAIRMAN: We don't want you to be on trial.

MR. STRIPLING: Mr. Lawson, how long have you been a member of the Screen Writers Guild?

MR. LAWSON: Since it was founded in its present form, in 1933.

MR. STRIPLING: Have you ever held any office in the guild?

MR. LAWSON: The question of whether I have held office is also a question which is beyond the purview of this Committee.

(*The Chairman pounding gavel.*)

MR. LAWSON: It is an invasion of the right of association under the Bill of Rights of this country.

THE CHAIRMAN: Please be responsive to the question.

MR. LAWSON: It is also a matter—

(*The Chairman pounding gavel.*)

MR. LAWSON:—of public record—

THE CHAIRMAN: You asked to be heard. Through your attorney, you asked to be heard, and we want you to be heard. And if you don't care to be heard, then we will excuse you, and we will put the record in without your answers.

MR. LAWSON: I wish to frame my own answers to your questions, Mr. Chairman, and I intend to do so.

THE CHAIRMAN: And you will be responsive to the questions or you will be excused from the witness stand.

MR. LAWSON: I will frame my own answers, Mr. Chairman.

THE CHAIRMAN: Go ahead, Mr. Stripling.

MR. STRIPLING: I repeat the question, Mr. Lawson: Have you ever held any position in the Screen Writers Guild?

MR. LAWSON: I stated that it is outside the purview of the rights of this Committee to inquire into any form of association—

THE CHAIRMAN: The Chair will determine what is in the purview of this Committee.

MR. LAWSON: My rights as an American citizen are no less than the responsibilities of this Committee of Congress.

THE CHAIRMAN: Now, you are just making a big scene for yourself and getting all "het up." (*Laughter.*) Be responsive to the questioning, just the same as all the witnesses have. You are no different from the rest. Go ahead, Mr. Stripling.

MR. LAWSON: I am being treated differently from the rest.

THE CHAIRMAN: You are not being treated differently.

MR. LAWSON: Other witnesses have made statements, which included quotations from books, references to material which had no connection whatsoever with the interest of this Committee.

THE CHAIRMAN: We will determine whether it has connection. Now, you go ahead—

MR. LAWSON: It is absolutely beyond the power of this Committee to inquire into my association in any organization.

THE CHAIRMAN: Mr. Lawson, you will have to stop or you will leave the witness stand. And you will leave the witness stand because you are in contempt. That is why you will leave the witness stand. And if you are just trying to force me to put you in contempt, you won't have to try much harder. You know what has happened to a lot of people that have been in contempt of this Committee this year, don't you?

MR. LAWSON: I am glad you have made it perfectly clear that you are going to threaten and intimidate the witnesses, Mr. Chairman.

(*The Chairman pounding gavel.*)

MR. LAWSON: I am an American and I am not at all easy to intimidate, and don't think I am.

(*The Chairman pounding gavel.*)

MR. STRIPLING: Mr. Lawson, I repeat the question. Have you ever held any position in the Screen Writers Guild?

MR. LAWSON: I have stated that the question is illegal. But it is a matter of public record that I have held many offices in the Screen Writers Guild. I was its first president in 1933, and

I have held office on the board of directors of the Screen Writers Guild at other times.

A Summary of Lawson's Career

MR. STRIPLING: You have been employed in the motion-picture industry, have you not?

MR. LAWSON: I have.

MR. STRIPLING: Would you state some of the studios where you have been employed?

MR. LAWSON: Practically all of the studios, all the major studios.

MR. STRIPLING: As a screen writer?

MR. LAWSON: That is correct.

MR. STRIPLING: Would you list some of the pictures which you have written the script for?

MR. LAWSON: I must state again that you are now inquiring into the freedom of press and communications, over which you have no control whatsoever. You don't have to bring me here three thousand miles to find out what pictures I have written. The pictures that I have written are very well known. They are such pictures as *Action in the North Atlantic, Sahara*—

MR. STRIPLING: Mr. Lawson—

MR. LAWSON:—such pictures as *Blockade,* of which I am very proud, and in which I introduced the danger that this democracy faced from the attempt to destroy democracy in Spain in 1937. These matters are all matters of public record.

MR. STRIPLING: Mr. Lawson, would you object if I read a list of the pictures, and then you can either state whether or not you did write the scripts?

MR. LAWSON: I have no objection at all.

MR. STRIPLING: Did you write *Dynamite,* by M-G-M?

MR. LAWSON: I preface my answer, again, by saying that it is outside of the province of this Committee, but it is well known that I did.

MR. STRIPLING: *The Sea Bat,* by M-G-M?

MR. LAWSON: It is well known that I did.

MR. STRIPLING: *Success at Any Price,* RKO?

MR. LAWSON: Yes, that is from a play of mine, *Success Story.*

MR. STRIPLING: *Party Wire,* Columbia?

MR. LAWSON: Yes, I did.

MR. STRIPLING: *Blockade,* United Artists, Wanger?

MR. LAWSON: That is correct.

MR. STRIPLING: *Algiers,* United Artists, Wanger?

MR. LAWSON: Correct.

MR. STRIPLING: *Earth Bound,* Twentieth Century–Fox.

MR. LAWSON: Correct.

MR. STRIPLING: *Counterattack,* Columbia.

MR. LAWSON: Correct.

MR. STRIPLING: You have probably written others, have you not, Mr. Lawson?

MR. LAWSON: Many others. You have missed a lot of them.

MR. STRIPLING: You don't care to furnish them to the Committee, do you?

MR. LAWSON: Not in the least interested.

Stripling Asks About Communism Directly

MR. STRIPLING: Mr. Lawson, are you now or have you ever been a member of the Communist Party of the United States?

MR. LAWSON: In framing my answer to that question I must emphasize the points that I have raised before. The question of Communism is in no way related to this inquiry, which is an attempt to get control of the screen and to invade the basic rights of American citizens in all fields.

MR. MCDOWELL: Now, I must object—

MR. STRIPLING: Mr. Chairman—

(*The Chairman pounding gavel.*)

MR. LAWSON: The question here relates not only to the question of my membership in any political organization, but this Committee is attempting to establish the right—

(*The Chairman pounding gavel.*)

MR. LAWSON:—which has been historically denied to any committee of this sort, to invade the rights and privileges and immunity of American citizens, whether they be Protestant, Methodist, Jewish, or Catholic, whether they be Republicans or Democrats or anything else.

THE CHAIRMAN (*pounding gavel*): Mr. Lawson, just quiet down again. Mr. Lawson, the most pertinent question that we can ask is whether or not you have ever been a member of the Communist Party. Now, do you care to answer that question?

MR. LAWSON: You are using the old technique, which was used in Hitler['s] Germany in order to create a scare here.—

THE CHAIRMAN (*pounding gavel*): Oh—

MR. LAWSON:—in order to create an entirely false atmosphere in which this hearing is conducted—

(*The Chairman pounding gavel.*)

MR. LAWSON:—in order that you can then smear the motion-picture industry, and you can proceed to the press, to any form of communication in this country.

THE CHAIRMAN: You have learned—

MR. LAWSON: The Bill of Rights was established precisely to prevent the operation of any committee which could invade the basic rights of Americans. Now, if you want to know—

MR. STRIPLING: Mr. Chairman, the witness is not answering the question.

MR. LAWSON: If you want to know—

(*The Chairman pounding gavel.*)

MR. LAWSON:—about the perjury that has been committed here and the perjury that is planned—

THE CHAIRMAN: Mr. Lawson—

MR. LAWSON:—permit me and my attorneys to bring in here the witnesses that testified last week and permit us to cross-examine these witnesses, and we will show up the whole tissue of lies—

THE CHAIRMAN (*pounding gavel*): We are going to get the answer to that question if we have to stay here for a week. Are you a member of the Communist Party, or have you ever been a member of the Communist Party?

MR. LAWSON: It is unfortunate and tragic that I have to teach this Committee the basic principles of American—

THE CHAIRMAN (*pounding gavel*): That is not the question. That is not the question. The question is: Have you ever been a member of the Communist Party?

MR. LAWSON: I am framing my answer in the only way in which any American citizen can frame his answer to a question which absolutely invades his rights.

THE CHAIRMAN: Then you refuse to answer that question; is that correct?

MR. LAWSON: I have told you that I will offer my beliefs, affiliations, and everything else to the American public, and they will know where I stand.

THE Chairman (*pounding gavel*): Excuse the witness—

MR. LAWSON: As they do from what I have written.

THE CHAIRMAN (*pounding gavel*): Stand away from the stand—

MR. LAWSON: I have written Americanism for many years, and I shall continue to fight for the Bill of Rights, which you are trying to destroy.

THE CHAIRMAN: Officers, take this man away from the stand—

(*Applause and boos.*)

THE CHAIRMAN (*pounding gavel*): There will be no demonstrations. No demonstrations, for or against. Everyone will please be seated. All right, go ahead, Mr. Stripling. Proceed.

The Red Scare Is Un-American

Margaret Chase Smith

Margaret Chase Smith served in Congress for thirty-three years—including four terms in the Senate—from 1940 to 1973. She also became the first female presidential candidate from a major political party in 1964, when she received twenty-seven nominating votes at the Republican National Convention. The moment for which she is perhaps best known, though, occurred relatively early in her political career, in 1950—her second year in the Senate—when she delivered a fifteen-minute speech in opposition to the tactics of fellow senator Joseph McCarthy. Speaking for herself and six of her Republican colleagues, she delivered a "Declaration of Conscience" that, without naming McCarthy specifically, denounced his brand of anti-Communist activity as un-American. While her speech is at times unmistakably partisan—she repeatedly condemns the behaviors of the Democratic administration of Harry Truman—she also uttered one of the most memorable phrases of the Red Scare when she stated, "I do not want to see the Republican party ride to political victory on the Four Horsemen of Calumny—Fear, Ignorance, Bigotry, and Smear." As might be expected, McCarthy issued a harsh response to Smith's rebuke, referring contemptuously to the seven cosigners of the declaration as "Snow White and the Six Dwarfs." The principles of the declaration are tempered somewhat by the fact that all seven of its signers voted later in 1950 to reject the Tydings Committee's findings that McCarthy's charges

Margaret Chase Smith, address to the U.S. Senate, Washington, DC, June 1, 1950.

of Communist infiltration of the State Department were unfounded. Nevertheless, Smith's statement became a symbol of resistance to the Red Scare.

Mr. President [Smith is addressing her speech, as is customary to the President of the Senate], I would like to speak briefly and simply about a serious national condition. It is a national feeling of fear and frustration that could result in national suicide and the end of everything that we Americans hold dear. It is a condition that comes from the lack of effective leadership either in the legislative branch or the executive branch of our government.

That leadership is so lacking that serious and responsible proposals are being made that national advisory commissions be appointed to provide such critically needed leadership.

I speak as briefly as possible because too much harm has already been done with irresponsible words of bitterness and selfish political opportunism. I speak as simply as possible because the issue is too great to be obscured by eloquence. I speak simply and briefly in the hope that my words will be taken to heart.

Mr. President, I speak as a Republican. I speak as a woman. I speak as a United States senator. I speak as an American.

A Forum of Hate and Character Assassination

The United States Senate has long enjoyed worldwide respect as the greatest deliberative body in the world. But recently that deliberative character has too often been debased to the level of a forum of hate and character assassination sheltered by the shield of congressional immunity.

It is ironical that we senators can in debate in the Senate, directly or indirectly, by any form of words, impute to any American who is not a senator any conduct or motive unworthy or unbecoming an American—and without that non-senator American having any legal redress against us—yet if we say the same thing in the Senate about our colleagues we can be stopped on the grounds of being out of order.

It is strange that we can verbally attack anyone else without restraint and with full protection, and yet we hold ourselves above the same type of criticism here on the Senate floor. Surely the United States Senate is big enough to take self-criticism and self-appraisal. Surely we should be able to take the same kind of character attacks that we "dish out" to outsiders.

I think that it is high time for the United States Senate and its members to do some real soul searching and to weigh our consciences as to the manner in which we are performing our duty to the people of America and the manner in which we are using or abusing our individual powers and privileges.

I think that it is high time that we remembered that we have sworn to uphold and defend the Constitution. I think that it is high time that we remembered that the Constitution, as amended, speaks not only of the freedom of speech but also of trial by jury instead of trial by accusation.

Whether it be a criminal prosecution in court or a character prosecution in the Senate, there is little practical distinction when the life of a person has been ruined.

The Basic Principles of Americanism

Those of us who shout the loudest about Americanism in making character assassinations are all too frequently those who, by our own words and acts, ignore some of the basic principles of Americanism—

The right to criticize.

The right to hold unpopular beliefs.

The right to protest.

The right of independent thought.

The exercise of these rights should not cost one single American citizen his reputation or his right to a livelihood nor should he be in danger of losing his reputation or livelihood merely because he happens to know someone who holds unpopular beliefs. Who of us does not? Otherwise none of us could call our souls our own. Otherwise thought control would have set in.

The American people are sick and tired of being afraid to speak their minds lest they be politically smeared as "Communists" or "Fascists" by their opponents. Freedom of speech is not what it used to be in America. It has been so abused by some that it is not exercised by others.

The American people are sick and tired of seeing innocent people smeared and guilty people whitewashed. But there have been enough proved cases, such as the *Amerasia* case, the [Alger] Hiss case, the Coplon case, and the Gold case, to cause nationwide distrust and strong suspicion that there may be something to the unproved, sensational accusations.[1]

A Challenge to the Republican Party

As a Republican, I say to my colleagues on this side of the aisle that the Republican party faces a challenge today that is not unlike the challenge which it faced back in Lincoln's day. The Republican party so successfully met that challenge that it emerged from the Civil War as the champion of a united nation—in addition to being a party which unrelentingly fought loose spending and loose programs.

Today our country is being psychologically divided by the confusion and the suspicions that are bred in the United States Senate to spread like cancerous tentacles of "know nothing, suspect everything" attitudes. Today we have a Democratic administration which has developed a mania for loose spending and loose programs. History is repeating itself—and the Republican party again has the opportunity to emerge as the champion of unity and prudence. The record of the present Democratic administration has provided us with sufficient campaign issues without the necessity of resorting to political smears. America is rapidly losing its position as leader of the world simply because the Democratic administration has pitifully failed to provide effective leadership.

The Democratic administration has completely confused the American people by its daily contradictory grave warnings

1. *Amerasia* was a pro-Communist publication in whose New York office a number of classified government documents were found. The editor and two foreign service officers were arrested but never brought to trial. In March 1950 Judith Coplon was found guilty of attempted espionage against the United States. In 1950, with a number of others, Harry Gold was arrested and convicted of passing American atomic secrets to the USSR.

and optimistic assurances, which show the people that our Democratic administration has no idea of where it is going.

The Democratic administration has greatly lost the confidence of the American people by its complacency to the threat of communism here at home and the leak of vital secrets to Russia through key officials of the Democratic administration. There are enough proved cases to make this point without diluting our criticism with unproved charges.

Surely these are sufficient reasons to make it clear to the American people that it is time for a change and that a Republican victory is necessary to the security of the country. Surely it is clear that this nation will continue to suffer so long as it is governed by the present ineffective Democratic administration.

The Four Horsemen of Calumny

Yet to displace it with a Republican regime embracing a philosophy that lacks political integrity or intellectual honesty would prove equally disastrous to the nation. The nation sorely needs a Republican victory. But I do not want to see the Republican party ride to political victory on the Four Horsemen of Calumny—Fear, Ignorance, Bigotry, and Smear.

I doubt if the Republican party could do so, simply because I do not believe the American people will uphold any political party that puts political exploitation above national interest. Surely we Republicans are not that desperate for victory.

I do not want to see the Republican party win that way. While it might be a fleeting victory for the Republican party, it would be a more lasting defeat for the American people. Surely it would ultimately be suicide for the Republican party and the two-party system that has protected our American liberties from the dictatorship of a one-party system.

As members of the minority party, we do not have the primary authority to formulate the policy of our government. But we do have the responsibility of rendering constructive criticism, of clarifying issues, of allaying fears by acting as responsible citizens.

As a woman, I wonder how the mothers, wives, sisters, and daughters feel about the way in which members of their families have been politically mangled in Senate debate—and I use the word "debate" advisedly.

Irresponsible Sensationalism

As a United States senator, I am not proud of the way in which the Senate has been made a publicity platform for irresponsible sensationalism. I am not proud of the reckless abandon in which unproved charges have been hurled from this side of the aisle. I am not proud of the obviously staged, undignified countercharges which have been attempted in retaliation from the other side of the aisle.

I do not like the way the Senate has been made a rendezvous for vilification, for selfish political gain at the sacrifice of individual reputations and national unity. I am not proud of the way we smear outsiders from the floor of the Senate and hide behind the cloak of congressional immunity and still place ourselves beyond criticism on the floor of the Senate.

As an American, I am shocked at the way Republicans and Democrats alike are playing directly into the Communist design of "confuse, divide, and conquer." As an American, I do not want a Democratic administration "whitewash" or "coverup" any more than I want a Republican smear or witch hunt.

As an American, I condemn a Republican Fascist just as much as I condemn a Democrat Communist. I condemn a Democrat Fascist just as much as I condemn a Republican Communist. They are equally dangerous to you and me and to our country. As an American, I want to see our nation recapture the strength and unity it once had when we fought the enemy instead of ourselves.

It is with these thoughts that I have drafted what I call a Declaration of Conscience. I am gratified that the senator from New Hampshire [Mr. Tobey], the senator from Vermont [Mr. Aiken], the senator from Oregon [Mr. Morse], the senator from New York [Mr. Ives], the senator from Minnesota [Mr. Thye], and the senator from New Jersey [Mr. Hendrickson] have concurred in that declaration and have authorized me to announce their concurrence.

The declaration reads as follows:

Statement of Seven Republican Senators

1. We are Republicans. But we are Americans first. It is as Americans that we express our concern with the growing confusion that threatens the security and stability of our country. Democrats and Republicans alike have contributed to that confusion.

2. The Democratic administration has initially created the confusion by its lack of effective leadership, by its contradictory grave warnings and optimistic assurances, by its complacency to the threat of communism here at home, by its oversensitiveness to rightful criticism, by its petty bitterness against its critics.

3. Certain elements of the Republican party have materially added to this confusion in the hopes of riding the Republican party to victory through the selfish political exploitation of fear, bigotry, ignorance, and intolerance. There are enough mistakes of the Democrats for Republicans to criticize constructively without resorting to political smears.

4. To this extent, Democrats and Republicans alike have unwittingly, but undeniably, played directly into the Communist design of "confuse, divide, and conquer."

5. It is high time that we stopped thinking politically as Republicans and Democrats about elections and started thinking patriotically as Americans about national security based on individual freedom. It is high time that we all stopped being tools and victims of totalitarian techniques—techniques that, if continued here unchecked, will surely end what we have come to cherish as the American way of life.

Margaret Chase Smith, Maine
Charles W. Tobey, New Hampshire
George D. Aiken, Vermont
Wayne L. Morse, Oregon
Irving M. Ives, New York
Edward J. Thye, Minnesota
Robert C. Hendrickson, New Jersey

Hunting for Communists Is like Hunting for Witches

Arthur Miller

Arthur Miller is among the foremost American play-
wrights of the twentieth century. Although his career
spanned nearly sixty years, he is perhaps best remembered for his work during the late 1940s and early 1950s,
which included the plays *Death of a Salesman* and *The Crucible.* In this excerpt from an article that appeared in June
2000 in the British newspaper the *Guardian,* Miller discusses his role, both personal and artistic, in the Red Scare,
especially as it relates to the creation of *The Crucible.* Set
in seventeenth-century Salem, Massachusetts, during the
time of the infamous witch trials, *The Crucible* is an alle-
gory that suggests parallels between the witch-hunt of
the 1600s and the hysteria surrounding communism in
the twentieth century. Miller shares his recollections of
the national mood, his experiences with Hollywood's
self-censorship, his subpoena by the House Committee on
Un-American Activities in 1956 (three years after *The Crucible* premiered), and his reasons for writing a work of art
that attempted to respond to the politics of his time.
Miller's reminiscence is punctuated by the assertion that
the play still seems to resonate with audiences around the
world despite the end of the Red Scare, which he suggests
is a sign that the impulses that created both the Salem
Witch Trials and McCarthyism still exist within people.

Arthur Miller, "Are You Now or Were You Ever...?" *The Guardian,* June 17, 2000.
Copyright © 2000 by Guardian Publications Ltd. Reproduced by permission.

I t would probably never have occurred to me to write a play about the Salem witch trials of 1692 had I not seen some astonishing correspondences with that calamity in the America of the late [19]40s and early [19]50s. My basic need was to respond to a phenomenon which, with only small exaggeration, one could say paralyzed a whole generation and in a short time dried up the habits of trust and toleration in public discourse.

I refer to the anti-communist rage that threatened to reach hysterical proportions and sometimes did. I can't remember anyone calling it an ideological war, but I think now that that is what it amounted to. I suppose we rapidly passed over anything like a discussion or debate, and into something quite different, a hunt not just for subversive people, but for ideas and even a suspect language. The object was to destroy the least credibility of any and all ideas associated with socialism and communism, whose proponents were assumed to be either knowing or unwitting agents of Soviet subversion.

An ideological war is like guerrilla war, since the enemy is an idea whose proponents are not in uniform but are disguised as ordinary citizens, a situation that can scare a lot of people to death. To call the atmosphere paranoid is not to say that there was nothing real in the American-Soviet stand-off. But if there was one element that lent the conflict a tone of the inauthentic and the invented, it was the swiftness with which all values were forced in months to reverse themselves.

Death of a Salesman opened in February 1949 and was hailed by nearly every newspaper and magazine. Several movie studios wanted it and finally Columbia Pictures bought it, and engaged a great actor, Frederick March, to play Willy [Loman, the central character].

In two years or less, with the picture finished, I was asked by a terrified Columbia to sign an anti-communist declaration to ward off picket lines which the rightwing American Legion was threatening to throw across the entrances of theatres showing the film. In the phone calls that followed, the air of panic was heavy. It was the first intimation of what would soon follow. I declined to make any such statement, which I found demeaning; what right had any organisation to demand anyone's pledge of loyalty? I was sure the whole thing would soon go away; it was just too outrageous.

But instead of the problem disappearing, the studio actually made another film, a short to be shown with *Salesman*. This was called *The Life of a Salesman* and consisted of several lectures by City College School of Business professors— which boiled down to selling was a joy, one of the most gratifying and useful professions, and that Willy was simply a nut. Never in show-business history has a studio spent so much good money to prove that its feature film was pointless. In less than two years *Death of a Salesman* had gone from being a masterpiece to being a heresy, and a fraudulent one at that.

Miller's Impression of the Early Years of the Red Scare

In 1948-51, I had the sensation of being trapped inside a perverse work of art, one of those [artist M.C.] Escher constructs in which it is impossible to make out whether a stairway is going up or down. Practically everyone I knew stood within the conventions of the political left of centre; one or two were Communist party members, some were fellow-travellers, and most had had a brush with Marxist ideas or organisations. I have never been able to believe in the reality of these people being actual or putative traitors any more than I could be, yet others like them were being fired from teaching or jobs in government or large corporations. The surreality of it all never left me. We were living in an art form, a metaphor that had suddenly, incredibly, gripped the country.

In today's terms, the country had been delivered into the hands of the radical right, a ministry of free-floating apprehension toward anything that never happens in the middle of Missouri. It is always with us, this anxiety, sometimes directed towards foreigners, Jews, Catholics, fluoridated water, aliens in space, masturbation, homosexuality, or the Internal Revenue [Service]. But in the 50s any of these could be validated as real threats by rolling out a map of China. And if this seems crazy now, it seemed just as crazy then, but openly doubting it could cost you.

So in one sense *The Crucible* was an attempt to make life real again, palpable and structured. One hoped that a work of art might illuminate the tragic absurdities of an anterior work of art that was called reality, but was not. It was the very swiftness of the change that lent it this surreality. Only three or four years earlier an American movie audience, on seeing a newsreel of [Soviet leader Joseph] Stalin saluting the Red Army, would have applauded, for that army had taken the brunt of the Nazi onslaught [in WWII], as most people were aware. Now they would look on with fear or at least bewilderment, for the Russians had become the enemy of mankind, a menace to all that was good. It was the Germans who, with amazing rapidity, were turning good. Could this be real? . . .

As for the idea of willingly subjecting my work not only to some party's discipline but to anyone's control, my repugnance was such that, as a young and indigent writer, I had turned down lucrative offers to work for Hollywood studios because of a revulsion at the thought of someone owning the paper I was typing on. It was not long, perhaps four or five years, before the fraudulence of Soviet cultural claims was as clear to me as it should have been earlier. But I would never have found it believable, in the 50s or later, that with its thuggish self-righteousness and callous contempt for artists' freedoms, that the Soviet way of controlling culture could be successfully exported to America.

Some greatly talented people were driven out of the US to work in England: screenwriters like Carl Foreman and Donald Ogden Stewart, actors like Charlie Chaplin and Sam Wanamaker. I no longer recall the number of our political exiles, but it was more than too many and disgraceful for a nation prideful of its democracy. . . .

It is not easy to convey the American fear of a masterful communism. The quickness with which Soviet-style regimes had taken over eastern Europe and China was breathtaking, and I believe it stirred up a fear in Americans of our own ineptitudes, our mystifying inability, despite our military victories, to control the world whose liberties we had so recently won back from the Axis powers.

Miller's Testimony Before HUAC

In 1956, the House Un-American Activities Committee (HUAC) subpoenaed me—I was cited for contempt of Congress for refusing to identify writers I had met at one of the two communist writers' meetings I had attended many years before. By then, the tide was going out for HUAC and it was finding it more difficult to make front pages. However, the news of my forthcoming marriage to Marilyn Monroe was too tempting to be passed. That our marriage had some connection with my being subpoenaed was confirmed when Chairman Walters [that is, Francis Walter] of the HUAC sent word to Joseph Rauh, my lawyer, that he would be inclined to cancel my hearing if Miss Monroe would consent to have a picture taken with him.

The offer having been declined, the good chairman, as my hearing came to an end, entreated me to write less tragically about our country. This lecture cost me $40,000 in lawyer's fees, a year's suspended sentence for contempt of Congress, and a $500 fine. Not to mention about a year of inaction in my creative life.

My fictional view of the period, my sense of its unreality had been, like any impotence, a psychologically painful experience. A similar paralysis descended on Salem. In both places, to keep social unity intact, the authority of leaders had to be hardened and words of scepticism toward them constricted. A new cautionary diction, an uncustomary prudence inflected our way of talking to one another. The word *socialism* was all but taboo. Words had gotten fearsome. As I learned directly in Ann Arbor [Michigan] on a 1953 visit, university students were avoiding renting rooms in houses run by the housing cooperative for fear of being labelled communist, so darkly suggestive was the word *cooperative*. The head of orientation at the university told me, in a rather cool, uninvolved manner, that the FBI was enlisting professors to report on students voicing leftwing opinions, and—more comedy—that they had also engaged students to report on professors with the same views. . . .

The heart of the darkness was the belief that a massive, profoundly organised conspiracy was in place and carried forward mainly by a concealed phalanx of intellectuals, including labour activists, teachers, professionals, sworn to undermine the American government. And it was precisely the invisibility of ideas that was frightening so many people. How could a play deal with this mirage world?

Paranoia breeds paranoia, but below paranoia there lies a bristling, unwelcome truth, so repugnant as to produce fantasies of persecution to conceal its existence. The unwelcome truth denied by the right was that the Hollywood writers accused of subversion were not a menace to the country, or even bearers of meaningful change. They wrote not propaganda but entertainment, some of it of a mildly liberal cast, but most of it mindless, or when it was political, as with [filmmakers] Preston Sturges or Frank Capra, entirely and exuberantly un-Marxist.

As for the left, its unacknowledged truth was more important for me. If nobody was being shot in our ideological war but merely vivisected by a headline, it struck me as odd, if understandable, that the accused were unable to cry out passionately their faith in the ideals of socialism. There were attacks on the HUAC's right to demand that a citizen reveal his political beliefs; but on the idealistic canon of their own convictions, the defendants were mute. The rare exception, like [singer/actor] Paul Robeson's declaration of faith in socialism as a cure for racism, was a rocket that lit up the sky.

The Origins of *The Crucible*

On a lucky afternoon I happened upon *The Devil in Massachusetts,* by Marion Starkey, a narrative of the Salem witch-hunt of 1692. I knew this story from my college reading, but in this darkened America it turned a completely new aspect toward me: the poetry of the hunt. Poetry may seem an odd word for a witch-hunt but I saw there was something of the marvellous in the spectacle of a whole village, if not an entire province, whose imagination was captured by a vision of something that wasn't there.

In time to come, the notion of equating the red-hunt with the witch-hunt would be condemned as a deception. There were communists and there never were witches. The deeper I moved into the 1690s, the further away drifted the America of the 1950s, and, rather than the appeal of analogy, I found something different to draw my curiosity and excitement.

Anyone standing up in the Salem of 1692 and denying that witches existed would have faced immediate arrest, the hardest interrogation and possibly the [hangman's] rope. Every authority not only confirmed the existence of witches but never questioned the necessity of executing them. It became obvious that to dismiss witchcraft was to forgo any understanding of how it came to pass that tens of thousands had been murdered as witches in Europe. To dismiss any relation between that episode and the hunt for subversives was to shut down an insight into not only the similar emotions but also the identical practices of both officials and victims.

There were witches, if not to most of us then certainly to everyone in Salem; and there were communists, but what was the content of their menace? That to me became the issue. Having been deeply influenced as a student by a Marxist approach to society, and having known Marxists and sympathizers, I could simply not accept that these people were spies or even prepared to do the will of the Soviets in some future crisis. That such people had thought to find hope of a higher ethic in the Soviet was not simply an American, but a worldwide, irony of catastrophic moral proportions, for their like could be found all over the world.

But as the 1950s dawned, they were stuck with the past. Part of the surreality of the anti-left sweep was that it picked up people for disgrace who had already turned away from a pro-Soviet past but had no stomach for naming others who had merely shared their illusions. But the hunt had captured some significant part of the American imagination and its power demanded respect.

Turning to Salem was like looking into a petri dish, an embalmed stasis with its principal moving forces caught in stillness. One had to wonder what the human imagination fed on that could inspire neighbours and old friends to emerge overnight as furies secretly bent on the torture and destruction of Christians. More than a political metaphor, more than a moral tale, *The Crucible,* as it developed over more than a year, became the awesome evidence of the power of human imagination inflamed, the poetry of suggestion, and the tragedy of heroic resistance to a society possessed to the point of ruin.

In the stillness of the Salem courthouse, surrounded by the images of the 1950s but with my head in 1692, what the two eras had in common gradually gained definition. Both had the menace of concealed plots, but most startling were the similarities in the rituals of defence, the investigative routines; 300 years apart, both prosecutions alleged membership of a secret, disloyal group. Should the accused confess, his honesty could only be proved by naming former confederates. The informer became the axle of the plot's existence and the investigation's necessity. . . .

Miller's View of the Play's Lasting Relevance

The Crucible is my most-produced play. It seems to be one of the few surviving shards of the so-called McCarthy period. And it is part of the play's history that, to people in so many parts of the world, its story seems to be their own. I used to think, half seriously, that you could tell when a dictator was about to take power, or had been overthrown, in a Latin American country, if *The Crucible* was suddenly being produced in that country. . . .

There is hardly a week that passes when I don't ask the unanswerable question: what am I now convinced of that will turn out to be ridiculous? And yet one can't forever stand on the shore; at some point, filled with indecision, scepticism, reservation and doubt, you either jump in or concede that life is forever elsewhere. Which, I dare say, was one of the major impulses behind the decision to attempt *The Crucible.*

Salem village, that pious, devout settlement at the edge of white civilization, had displayed three centuries before the Russo-American rivalry and the issues it raised—what can only be called a built-in pestilence in the human mind; a fatality forever awaiting the right conditions for its always unique, forever unprecedented outbreak of distrust, alarm, suspicion and murder. And for people wherever the play is performed on any of the five continents, there is always a certain amazement that the same terror that is happening to them or that is threatening them, has happened before to others. It is all very strange. But then, the Devil is known to lure people into forgetting what it is vital for them to remember—how else could his endless reappearances always come as such a marvellous surprise?

CHAPTER 3

The Cultural Effects of the Red Scare

Portrait of an
American Communist

John McPartland

Life magazine was one of the most widely read publications in the United States in 1948, a year in which the Cold War intensified and public awareness of Soviet-American tensions grew dramatically. As the wartime alliance between the United States and the Soviet Union disintegrated, suspicion of Communists in American society quickly arose again, stoked largely by political events such as the congressional hearings on Communist infiltration of Hollywood that were held in 1947. Despite this climate of mistrust, very few ordinary Americans actually had any first-hand knowledge of communism. *Life* published this article in its January 5, 1948, issue in part to give readers a sense of what a typical American Communist might be like. In describing the pseudonymous (and possibly fictional) "Kelly," journalist John McPartland attempts to draw a picture not of a leader in the movement but of an ordinary American youth motivated to become a Communist as much by his emotional insecurity—note the frequent references to women being used as lures in the description of Kelly's initiation—as by his political beliefs. While McPartland's description is hardly flattering or positive, it is also notable for its relative restraint in branding Kelly as merely misguided, rather than as a vicious enemy. Such a view was not shared by FBI director J. Edgar Hoover or anti-Communist crusader Joseph McCarthy, but this article may have been many Americans' first and possibly only experience with an everyday "Red" in their midst.

John McPartland, "Portrait of an American Communist," *Life,* vol. 31, January 5, 1948, pp. 75–82. Copyright © 1948 by Time, Inc. All rights reserved. Reproduced by permission.

He joined the party in 1935, when he was 20 years old. It wasn't simple, like joining the Democratic party or the Elks. It was the reward for three years of work, study and obedience to discipline. And he knew that separation from the party would be equally difficult; it would not be accomplished by tearing up a card and saying, "Count me out." Through the three years many people had given much thought to impressing him with the importance and completeness of party membership and party activity. The indoctrination had entered the marrow of his bones, dictated even the shape of his dreams.

It began when he was still a high-school student in Chicago as a social pleasure and what he thought then to be intellectual adventure. A party at Rae's house, a regular high school kids' party with kissing games and refreshments served by Rae's mother at 11 o'clock, was the official beginning of his activities on the fringes of the movement. The older fellows started a political discussion and he was impressed by their intentness, their verbal brilliancies and by the way the girls at the party admired them. He entered the discussion, fortified with an easily smiling face, an agile mind and an aggressiveness acquired through childhood years of family quarrels in an overcrowded flat. He was brash, the older boys made a fool of him by luring him into intellectual gambits already ancient to them, but he handled himself well, he did not lose his temper, he retreated and dodged without conceding. They marked him and he was invited to another party the following Sunday.

These wonderful people, illuminated and consumed by their own internal flames, fascinated him. He wanted to go with them, to model himself in their sardonic and idealistic images. It was not too hard to do—they even encouraged him. There were parties, picnics, beach suppers, all with songs and laughter, discussions and admiring girls. A magic seemed to be operating. Each time he was welcomed as a fine fellow by these suave intellectuals, pretty girls appeared and responded generously to his clumsy love-making. What more could a boy want than this?

Of course there was another side to all this. There were tasks, little ones first, more important ones later. He distributed literature at mass meetings, walked in a hunger march, and it was rather fun, even a little exciting. He did not notice that he was being watched by the older men, watched for ability and obedience.

Soon he was attending the Workers' School three evenings a week. One or two evenings he worked on party activities— wrapping newspapers at the print shop, attending mass meetings, picketing the mass meetings of other organizations. The remaining evenings were devoted to the satisfactions of coffee and cigarets until 3 in the morning at a little cafeteria with other boys and girls of the movement, young law students, smooth college girls; beer and sandwiches in the parlor of a West Side flat with his friends; love-making in Douglas Park with a party girl.

These party girls were wonderful. They could talk with the best of the law students, they carried placards and fought policemen, they danced and went to bed. He didn't appreciate, at this time, that they went to bed in much the same way they carried placards—as a service to the party.

The Education of a Communist

The Workers' School was difficult, much more rigorous than a course in high-school math. The precisions of [Communist theorist Karl] Marx and the greater precisions of [Vladimir] Lenin and [Joseph] Stalin permitted no guesswork or bluffing. He learned the catechism, the patter, the terminology. After three months of the Workers' School he could spot a "supporter," a "diversionist" or a "dissenter" in a conversation on the weather. The anointed spoke only the approved words; to his amusement—in those days he still had a sense of humor—he found that he used the patter and the terminology even in his love-making.

Now he could hold up his end in the discussions over coffee and cigarets in the little cafeteria or through the impassioned arguments in the parlors of the little West Side flats. He quoted Lenin with the best of them, could tell the decisions of a party plenum, quote the *Pravda* [the official Soviet newspaper] of 1918. The older boys hid their condescension; they remembered the days when *they* had had only three months of the Workers' School, and besides, they would have been severely reprimanded by their cell leaders for injuring the morale of a likely prospect. Also, he was much in love with Sherry, a party girl, at this time, and all of the older boys, who shared a syndrome of memories about Sherry, regarded him as a little brother. He was very happy through this period.

These were great days. There was a sense of battle and of victory in the party. Fascism hovered like a thickening cloud over Europe and the world, and the party was the sword of the people, the banner of freedom or any other useful cliché you might think of. Some of "the best people" were banded to protect the rights of Communists.

And there was the enemy. Not the confused inheritors of unearned wealth, not the abashed bankers and bewildered businessmen, but the Lovestonites, the Trotskyites, the Cannonites, the Socialists [all rival leftist organizations] and a score of splinter parties. These were the heretics, the unclean, the Ishmaelites. He learned to despise them, destroy their literature and maybe, if circumstances seemed right, even engage them in physical battle.

He had his membership in the party. His parents, his relatives, the bustle of the stuffy family flat with its smells, its food, its comfort were far away now. His friends of school and the old neighborhood were forgotten—the party left no room for friendships or loyalties other than those of the party. He had a party name—"Kelly"—and he lived with his girl and another party couple in a third-floor flat in the intellectual slums near the University of Chicago.

"Kelly" Begins Working for the Cause

"Kelly" became a teacher on the Adult Education Project of the WPA [Work Projects Administration, a federal government program]. He earned $85 a month and worked about 14 hours a week in makeshift classrooms located in deteriorating settlement houses scattered through the industrial belt of the South Side. The party demands were much greater now—there was little time for cigarets and coffee, for the endless and circuitous arguments he had once enjoyed. He attended classes in parliamentary law. He bent over a Mimeograph [copying] machine for weary hours, he attended meetings in the Black Belt, in lodge halls over the taverns of the steel-mill district. He marched, he picketed, he broke up street-corner meetings of the damned Trotskyites. Sometimes his girl was with him, often she was gone for days at a time. When she was away he sometimes slept with the other girl while the man slept alone.

He was never lonely. The telephone of the flat rang frequently and there would be party gossip, party scandal— "Mike's been thrown out of the cell because he's a disrupter, a Lovestonite, a counterrevolutionary and a homosexual." He learned that the mortality of party memberships was high, there were endless suspicions, testings and tricks to discover the quality of true believers. Expulsions were matters of excitement and gabbling, always ending with the party dictum that the unfortunate was a moral leper as well as a political dullard. Invariably those jettisoned by the party were stigmatized as homosexuals, drug addicts, police informers and syphilitics. During this period "Kelly" believed these charges to be the simple truth and was considerably concerned over his failure to have detected such moral, physical and mental lesions in people he had known so well.

"Kelly" Learns About the Party Line

A touch of bitterness developed in his party relationships at this time, the product of a series of important political operations directed by the distant and unfathomable masters of the Communist party. First was his disappointment over the Steel Workers' Organizing Committee. [Labor leader] John L. Lewis, who has a shrewd insight into the qualities of leadership, needed, in those years, men of ability, integrity and courage to organize the manifold clusterings of the Committee for Industrial Organization. While he may have hated the Communist party as the devil hates holy water he knew that for his purposes at this time the party could supply him with the men he wanted. He took them as organizers, and with them received the blessings of the party. "Kelly" had been taught in his labor history that Lewis was an enemy of the working class, a collaborator with the operators, a fascist, a monomanic and a counterrevolutionary. Now he was taught that Lewis was a kindly liberal, a fighter on the side of the masses. "Kelly" had only a little trouble in correcting his perspective on Lewis. It was much the same kind of evolution that occurred in the case of Franklin Roosevelt, once pictured as a leering, top-hatted oppressor, a consort of Wall Street and the bankers but later to receive the stamp of party approval. These changes were frequent, and "Kelly" was getting used to them. The party line might whip about like a lariat, but he believed that behind its curves and loops there was an all-seeing wisdom that, in time and with much sacrifice, would bring about the redemption of the people of the world.

At the time "Kelly" was still too naive to appreciate the involved machinations that brought the party and John L. Lewis into a sort of gavotte [a dance] in which each bowed, walked toward the other, bowed and walked away again, but he was not too naive to know that the party had inserted a number of organizers into the Steel Workers' Organizing Committee in the local area. Despite his record of discipline, obedience and attendance at all party educational programs, he had not been one of them. He did not know that this disappointment was also a matter of strategy, that he was to be subjected to a series of ever greater disappointments until his response could no longer be questioned. He was a marked man, described in sealed and cryptic correspondence that had placed his name, biographical data, psychological evaluation, educational and organizational history in an envelope of a special bureau in Moscow. The next few years were intended to be bad, trying years for "Kelly": only the strong deserve responsibility.

The Massacre at Republic Steel

Then came the shock of the massacre, a shock which, if it had been noticed by the cold-eyed men in a little tavern near the Republic Steel works in South Chicago, might have meant the end of "Kelly's" career in the Communist party. This was the spring [1937] of the "Little Steel" strike, a strike which had shut down the furnaces of proud Tom Girdler, head of Republic Steel. This was the time of the "Republic massacre."

The striking steelworkers, friends and sympathizers who marched across the field before the Republic plant believed they were making a peaceable demonstration. They expected no serious trouble and intended to cause no serious trouble. In front of the strikebound plant stood a line of armed policemen. "Kelly" knew what the marching men did not know— that the party was doing its best to provoke a massacre. Already the party had prepared a first-aid station, the existence of which was unknown to the strikers and their friends, in an abandoned tavern near the mill. "Kelly" knew that the party tacticians counted on being able to provoke the police into opening fire without cause. The party was right, the police fired, the march broke into a panicked rout, and 10 men died as a result. It was a fine massacre from the standpoint of the party. It took "Kelly" some little time to "rationalize" the Republic massacre and see the party's wisdom. It was well for him that his momentary doubts were not noticed.

Another thing that tended to embitter "Kelly" was more personal. The party line, the dicta which determined every activity and every thought of a party member, had always been clear and precise on the subject of racial equality. When he had first become involved in the social activities that fringed the party, "Kelly" attended the interracial dances and beach parties which were mandatory enjoyment for the faithful. "Kelly" appreciated the importance of interracial affairs: they gave proof that the party was the organization of humanity, without prejudice or discrimination; they welcomed the Negro population into the party fold, like a great dark fruit, ripe and ready to fall into waiting hands. . . .

Spain: Another Disappointment for "Kelly"

He wanted to go to Spain. The party was recruiting men to fight on the Loyalist side [in the Spanish civil war, 1936–1939] although "Kelly" was politically adept enough to know now that once in Spain these men would do much of their fighting against the Anarcho-Syndicalists, against every tinge of politi-

cal faith that varied from the razor-sharp line of party recti-
tude. But he wanted to go—to find escape from the monotony
of discipline, from the fear of expulsion—but they would not
let him go. Others went, to die or to come back swaggering in
their berets. Some returned as bitter postgraduates, ready for
any party order; others as haunted men, believing in nothing.
"Kelly" stayed, picketed, marched, talked, wrapped his papers
and found that political maturity was setting in.

He discovered that his studies of parliamentary law, ordered
by the party, were highly useful. A union local of four or five
hundred members could easily be dominated by a dozen party
adherents. It was much like manipulating puppets—a party
man popped up and made a motion, somebody of the "unor-
ganized" would try to say something and three party people
talked around him, talked him down. Before long the party
would control the officers of the union and through them control the union's policy. It was so simple that it made him con-
temptuous of the rank and file. Let the workers keep their
place, let their destiny be managed by trained and capable people. And where else were there experts in the management of
people for a distant good but in the Communist party?

"Kelly" was intelligent. He realized that beneath the announced party line there was the real program, and while the
line seemed to veer and reverse itself the real program was un-
changing or, rather, changing slowly, like the movement of a
glacier slipping down a broad valley. It was when he was sent
to Detroit to work in the great factional battle of the West Side
local of the U.A.W. [United Auto Workers] that he began to
sense that the program of the party was not concerned with
evanescent good, not with little luxuries or little comforts for
the workers even though it might use such picayune [minor] re-
wards as lures to accomplish its immediate purposes; the program of the party was planned in terms of decades, in the
course of which the party intended to advance the Soviet Union
as the only possible control for the people of the world. With
this rationalization he was able to back and fill, change course,
spin and stop, in the U.A.W. No infantry private in a Prussian
regiment was ever more responsive to orders than "Kelly" was.

His own life made sense to him only if he banished all questioning of the rightness of the party. Accepting the simple dogma that the party was always right made his life right, gave him a full satisfaction in living. He followed the party law: "Those who are not with us are against us." To "Kelly," as to any other trusted member of the party, being "with" them meant following every order, taking each contradiction without question.

"Kelly" had become well-educated in social history. He appreciated the similarity between the party and certain orders of the Catholic Church in their ruthless demands upon the individual; he justified the parallel by assuming that discipline in itself was good but that only the party had adapted discipline to a necessary and inevitable program. By now, after several years of slavery to the party, of following its commands in every aspect of his life, he was aware that he was no longer an individual. He was a party member.

By 1939 he had found the power to hate coldly, to despise, to make decisions that reflected only the dictates of the party line. He sat in the meeting in that black week that was to have been the great jubilee, celebrating the 20th anniversary of the Communist party, the week of the announcement of the German-Soviet pact. [American Communist leader] Earl Browder spoke to the 12,000 that sat beneath the mocking banners which decried the "Munichmen" [i.e., Germans and their sympathizers] beneath the pictures of Washington, Lincoln, Lenin and Stalin. "Kelly" was there with his wife—the party had indicated that the line now approved of marriage—and behind him were Trotskyites come to jeer the party.

"Poor Browder," they said, laughing, "he doesn't know what to say. He hasn't got the word from Moscow yet."

"Why is Browder like the Brooklyn Bridge?"

"Because he depends on cables [i.e., telegrams]."

"Kelly" didn't smile. He turned around, looked, his face passive, and turned to the front again. He would not forget those two faces.

He sat through the empty coldness when, after the conclusion of Browder's floundering talk, the party asked for contributions, and organizations that had been in the practice of giving substantial checks sat silent, suspicious, unfriendly.

The Long Road

The year followed when the line preached "imperialist war," and "Kelly" sang "The Yanks Aren't Coming" in the almost deserted meetings. The time came when once again the war was a fight for freedom, a fight against fascism. "Kelly" was far beyond questioning. He sat in the little meetings and listened to the quiet talk of men who, like him, had come the long road. When he spoke the others listened, he was accepted, he was trusted. Behind him were the gay beach parties, the songs, the cigarets and coffee, the intellectual arguments, the girls, the pamphlets, the parades, the Maxwell Street Station, the bruises from night sticks, the 10 dead on the prairie in front of Republic Steel, the brown baby Sheila had given to its Negro grandparents, the tiredness, the drumbeat of dogma, the curving, swerving, omniscient line. "Kelly" was a Communist, with a dossier that listed him as "reliable." He did what the party told him to do. He could be allowed to suggest ways and means; it was known that he would never question the directive.

He was drafted. The instructions from the inconspicuous, tight-lipped man who ran the party were to be a good soldier, to try for a commission and to keep politically "clean."

The Army fixed his rotted teeth, put 20 solid pounds on him, straightened his slumped shoulders and made a more useful Communist out of him. He learned to be direct and aggressive; he became a corporal, a sergeant, and then he was selected for officer candidate school at Fort Benning, Ga.

Counter-Intelligence held up his appointment. His fingerprints were in the files and he was carded as a known agitator. "Kelly" was called before the S-2 [military security] officer of his training camp. They talked for an hour; "Kelly" sounded straightforward; he said he was a liberal, a Democrat and never a party member. The S-2 recommended clearing him and a few months later "Kelly" was an infantry second lieutenant.

He was a "book" officer, strict, demanding, following regulations with scrupulous accuracy. When the war ended he was a captain, a Third Army veteran with an excellent combat record. During his three and a half years of service his only party business was to be a good soldier. True, as a corporal he had been the man selected in his company to send weekly reports of any political dissension in the barracks to a masked address in a nearby town, but here he had been on the Army's side, one of their casually selected, lowest-echelon G-2 agents. This had amused him.

Later in 1945, the party had a new directive—"Agitate openly for immediate demobilization." The honeymoon was over. "Kelly" went to work, and the enlisted men of his command were pleasantly surprised, to find their martinet captain suddenly encouraging their efforts toward the separation center. In the Philippines a party friend of his, a sergeant, worked up a series of gigantic demonstrations protesting slow demobilization in the Pacific. It was an easy directive, the GIs [enlisted troops] wanted out anyway, but "Kelly" worked at it as methodically as he had organized years earlier.

"Kelly" Waits

Out of the Army, "Kelly" discovered the war had brought changes in party activities. No more "hunger marches," no more organizing battles—the party wanted its members to get jobs, acquire respectability. "Kelly" found a good job on the basis of his war record; he got a minor executive post in a factory and settled down with his wife in a pleasant suburban home.

If he wanted to leave the party this was his opportunity. The strong hold of using every bit of his time, of dictating his every acquaintance and his every action had been broken by the Army years. For the first time in a decade he was a free man—but he did not want to be free.

The high-level policy of the party now was to prepare for a coming period of economic chaos and, if possible, to hurry it along. The party had a plan of action. Most of the men like "Kelly" were to lie low, keep out of trouble and keep out of sight. These were the trusted men who no longer needed the interminable indoctrination and testing. When the time came they would step out in front and openly become the party's leaders. A second group was to act as stalking horses, parading their party affiliation and protesting any action against them as an invasion of civil liberties. A third group, the new members and the older members who had not proved themselves, was to work openly for various projects of civic betterment.

So "Kelly" waits. Once a week he attends a closed meeting of the party and there is a discussion of plans, policies and directives. He is convinced that 1932 [i.e., an economic crisis that stimulates political dissent] will come again, that the U.S. will go into a tailspin and that we may go to war against the Soviet Union. There is no question of divided loyalties here—"Kelly" knows that he is an agent of the Commissariat of Foreign Affairs of the Soviet Union and he is proud of it. For, in addition to being the fanatic that years of party membership have made him, he also suffers from a common disease—someday maybe he, "Kelly," will have power, and he is becoming hungry for power. "Kelly" expects to lead protest marches again, he expects to hear the clatter of machine guns in American streets, and he believes this time of crisis to be only a few years away. Meanwhile he maintains his simple loyalty to the party line. Work against aiding Britain, work against the Marshall Plan, oppose any strengthening of our armed forces, fight the Taft-Hartley Act [a piece of anti-Communist legislation]—all these things can be done openly as an expression of a free democracy. The new members, the well-meaning hangers-on and the followers of the "do good" line will help in these directives—the deeper plans are not meant for them. The deeper plans are concerned with the bloody years that "Kelly" believes are part of America's future.

And "Kelly" is without humor. After the recent [1947] French elections made the right-wing Gaullists the largest party in France he shrugged off his disappointment. "Do you know," he asked, "that there are more members of the Communist party in France, proportionate to the population, than there are in the Soviet Union?"

Television Both Helped and Hindered McCarthyism

Thomas Rosteck

Thomas Rosteck is associate professor of communications at the University of Arkansas at Fayetteville. In the following excerpt, he writes about the relationship between McCarthyism and television, especially in terms of the groundbreaking documentary journalism program *See It Now,* which premiered in 1951. Rosteck first discusses the ways in which Senator Joseph McCarthy and other anti-Communist crusaders attempted to use the developing medium of television to their advantage in the early 1950s, in terms of both broadcasting their message to the public and gaining greater personal notoriety. He then proceeds to discuss how *See It Now,* a collaboration between producer Fred W. Friendly and journalist Edward R. Murrow, changed the nature of what was being shown on television. Rosteck argues that *See It Now* represents one of the first serious attempts at principled television journalism and analyzes the program's investigations of and discussion about McCarthyism in the early to mid-1950s as evidence to support this argument. He also argues that by sparking public curiosity, McCarthyism both directly and indirectly contributed to the rapid growth of the television industry in the first half of the 1950s.

Thomas Rosteck, *See It Now Confronts McCarthyism: Television Documentary and the Politics of Representation.* Tuscaloosa: University of Alabama Press, 1994. Copyright © 1994 by The University of Alabama Press. All rights reserved. Reproduced by permission.

For many Americans, the world had simply gone crazy. As a new decade began in 1950, the American mood was unsettled and uncertain. To perhaps a majority, the situation both at home and abroad seemed grim, forbidding, and sinister. Communism was a threat—an "evil shadow" hanging over the world, an implacable enemy threatening and powerful. Worldwide communism seemed to gain strength after the end of the Second World War and, no longer confined to Soviet Russia, proclaimed its public dedication to the annihilation of Western democracies.

In foreign affairs, the Communists, or "Reds," seemed voracious aggressors. Immediately after the war, to America's dismay, the Soviet Union consolidated its hold on the nations of Eastern Europe, establishing Socialist regimes apparently directed from Moscow. More disturbing still, nuclear war seemed somehow inevitable after 1949. When the Soviet Union successfully detonated an atomic bomb, and a few years later exploded a hydrogen device, America ceased to be the only nation with the fearsome nuclear weapon. In response, [President Harry] Truman, and later the [Dwight] Eisenhower administration, through the foreign aid program took an increasingly hard line against Communist aggression in Western Europe, in Greece, and in Turkey.

But these actions seemed less important to most Americans than the shocking fall of China to communism. Despite American aid and support in early 1950, the Nationalist Chinese forces of Chiang Kai-shek withdrew to the island of Taiwan, leaving mainland China to the Communist forces of Mao Tse-Tung. Only a few short months later, a public weary of war saw American men again in battle. This time, combat came in support of United Nations forces in Korea—a "police action" against a North Korean Communist invasion of the South. The undeclared war would drag on—influencing the public mood and domestic politics—for three and a half years.

During this era, many Americans sensed danger not only from the outside but also from within. "Spies" were exposed and arrested in many of the Western democracies, with results that fed fears, suspicions, and the perception that America was a beleaguered society under constant "attack" from traitors and turncoats. In England, a prominent scientist confessed that he had passed American atomic information to the Russians, and in the United States [FBI director] J. Edgar Hoover branded the American Communist party a "fifth column" [i.e., an internal threat] dedicated to the undermining of democracy. Throughout the postwar years, the House Committee on Un-American Activities made headlines with sensational charges of Communist infiltration—eventually launching a series of well-publicized hearings on subversive activities in the motion picture and entertainment industries. . . .

McCarthyism and the Media

Within this era of fear, the trajectories of the junior senator from Wisconsin [Joseph McCarthy] and the so-called Mc-Carthyism movement, of the newborn television industry, and of the *See It Now* television series intersected at several junctions long before the telecast of the *See It Now* programs on McCarthyism. In fact, the long and complex curve of their relationship reveals the pressures and counterpressures of the age. For it is more than coincidence that the early, formative years of the television industry coincided with the purge years at the height of McCarthyism. As the witch-hunt atmosphere grew unabated in the years 1948 through 1954, the fledgling medium was unavoidably shaped by it, and the effects of this era of McCarthyism upon the industry may be traced directly.

Blacklisting in the broadcast industry began with the first appearance of a broadside entitled *Counterattack: The Newsletter of Facts on Communism*. Appearing late in 1947, it was published by three former FBI agents: Theodore C. Kirkpatrick, Kenneth M. Bierly, and John G. Keenan—who called themselves American Business Consultants. The trio assembled back files of the *Daily Worker, New Masses,* and other [leftist] publications, along with the programs of rallies, fundraising appeals, organization letterheads, and other documents from "subversive" groups. From these sources, they compiled names of those mentioned and listed these people alongside "citations" of their "front" activities. Three years later, the

Consultants produced another list, this one focusing only upon the infant broadcasting industry.

Red Channels: The Report of Communist Influence in Radio and Television appeared in June 1950. In its preface, the pamphlet claimed that Communists relied on television and radio as their chief transmission "belts" to give pro-Sovietism to the American people. The book assigned "citations" to 151 people in the broadcasting media. The list included some of the most talented and admired people in the industry—mostly writers, directors, and performers.

Although its influence may seem difficult to understand today, *Red Channels* had enormous impact. Once it had been widely distributed, it was used as a reference before anyone was hired by any network, any producer, or any advertising agency for any job, even as a consultant. Scores of artists were denied employment by cautious network executives eager to avoid the semblance of impropriety, which might, they reasoned, invite increased political interference in the new "business" of television. Among the networks, the Columbia Broadcasting System (CBS) was especially zealous in institutionalizing blacklisting and established, in 1950, a sort of loyalty oath, followed in 1951 by the appointment of an executive specializing in security. At the National Broadcasting Corporation (NBC) the legal department assumed similar duties.

But these problems for the broadcasters were exacerbated by Senator McCarthy. From the very beginning of his rise, McCarthy seemed to understand the media and how they worked—and the senator demonstrated a talent for generating and sustaining publicity unmatched by any other politician of his era. McCarthy and his followers were especially dependent upon the press, notably the news organizations outside the District of Columbia and the large eastern cities, to carry their message to the people. [Historian] Edwin Bayley notes that by the height of McCarthy's power, the senator or his activities were featured in daily coverage, usually on page 1 and often in several stories in a single day, reaching a peak in 1954, when it was not unusual for a paper to carry fifteen to twenty stories a day in which McCarthy was the central figure. A like proportion of McCarthy stories figured in radio and television news. . . .

McCarthy Uses Television to Spread His Message

McCarthy began to turn the powerful new medium of television to his own direct advantage. The senator's first appearance on national television occurred in February 1950, during a Senate investigation of his charges of Communist subversion of the State Department—the same charges that had thrust him into the national spotlight. While the so-called Tydings subcommittee investigation of McCarthy's charges reached no conclusions largely because the senator shifted and reshifted the various charges and names of those involved, exposure on the national medium apparently persuaded the senator that television appeals could move public opinion, and McCarthy soon began appearing with some regularity on television in those days. He would demand "equal time" to answer supposed "attacks" on him, and he was careful to schedule the hearings of his own investigative subcommittee to take advantage of live television coverage. One such milestone in McCarthy's career and use of television occurred in November 1952. On the eve of the presidential election, the senator appeared in a prime-time speech attacking Adlai Stevenson, the Democratic nominee, and claiming that Stevenson had ties to "Red fronts." McCarthy's speech was subsequently denounced by Democrats and disavowed by Republicans. But the Senator won enormous publicity as a result—an outcome that must once and for all have confirmed for the McCarthyites the value of television as a way of reaching the public with their message by going "over the head" of the established political parties.

Another milestone in the senator's rise and his exploitation of television broadcasting occurred in February 1953. As a more or less direct warning to those in the broadcast industry, McCarthy announced an investigation of the Voice of America [an international radio network sponsored by the U.S. government] for the purpose of eliminating "mismanagement and subversion" in the agency. The charges of subversion were the most interesting and quickly became an argument about how to make propaganda, with McCarthy and his accusatory witnesses taking the position that anything less than complete denunciation of Communists and enthusiastic praise for anti-Communists was subversion. The hearings were carried intermittently on one or another of the networks and quickly became a national sensation, [as Bayley notes,] "with McCarthy bullying a series of defiant or cringing bureaucrats, mocking their protestations of innocence and sneering at their declarations of hatred for communism." Even when McCarthy turned to other, still more sensational matters, the Voice of America investigation had a disheartening effect upon industry insiders, who found themselves growing ever more wary of the increasing interest taken by the senator and his followers in the industry's access to the public. . . .

A New Type of Program

As the McCarthyites' interest in television was intensifying, a new "documentary" program, one that was to shape future perception of the role of news and public affairs television, quietly began. On Sunday afternoon, November 18, 1951, at 3:30 eastern standard time (EST) with little fanfare, CBS introduced *See It Now*. The result of a collaboration between a young producer, Fred W. Friendly, and Edward R. Murrow, the hero of World War II's Battle of Britain and one of the most respected news commentators of the day, *See It Now* evolved from Friendly's original inspiration of covering a variety of different news stories or features over the radio, an idea that was eventually transplanted to the new medium of television. With Murrow before the camera, the first episode opened with simultaneous views of the Golden Gate Bridge in San Francisco and New York's Brooklyn Bridge. As this image appeared, Murrow said: "For the first time in the history of man we are able to look out at both the Atlantic and Pacific coasts of this great country at the same time." And then he continued, "no journalistic age was ever given a weapon for truth with quite the same scope as this fledgling television." . . .

The series innovated with respect to both the way that television news documentary was produced and expectations regarding subject matter. Its production techniques were unique for the time, and *See It Now* was the first to shoot its own film for its own specific purposes rather than use film that had already been shot for the newsreels or the daily news programs or had been taken from archives. And unlike any other documentary of the time, *See It Now* sent its cameras out without a prepared script. According to its producers, the program always filmed with a sound track, never dubbed, never used actors, and never rehearsed an interview.

But more important, *See It Now* was innovative in the way that it handled controversy. In the tense days of McCarthyism, the series was novel for engaging controversial subject matter. [According to historian Alexander Kendrick in] its day, *See It Now* was "the dominant if not the only news documentary series dealing with the sensitive topics and issues." Contemporary historians [such as Kendrick] have said that Murrow and Friendly "endowed TV news with a sense of substance." Perhaps as a result, it is often held up [according to Raymond Carroll] as the most "courageous instance of broadcast journalism during the history of television." *See It Now* seemed able, as Friendly observed later, to "do controversy and get away with it." The program supplied to network television what Friendly called "conviction, controversy, and a point of view." . . .

See It Now Covers McCarthyism

The paths of Senator McCarthy and the *See It Now* series had first crossed directly when *See It Now* featured the senator in a four-minute segment broadcast in mid-December of 1951, its first month on the air. In format, the segment presaged the later "Report on Senator McCarthy" by presenting a contrasting series of McCarthy public statements. But the telecast received little notice at the time. A few months later, Murrow interviewed McCarthy live on the March 16, 1952, edition. The senator aroused Murrow's ire by ignoring his questions and instead attacking colleagues in the Congress for questioning his actions and his motives.

By the beginning of the 1953–1954 season the *See It Now* team had developed its techniques, approach, and style and began both to treat a wider range of subjects and to cover them in greater depth. Now consistently dealing with only one story in each thirty-minute episode, a typical telecast moved swiftly between filmed segments, Murrow's interviews with involved parties live on the air, and "follow-ups" on previous reports, to the concluding Murrow "tailpieces" that were frequently calls to citizen action or evidence of problems and their causes and possible solutions. Thus *See It Now* began to focus on controversial issues and provocative subjects such as health care and costs, the defense industry, and the relationship between smoking and lung cancer in a way that made the program influential with opinion leaders and helped television in those early years to become an indispensable medium.

It was inevitable, of course, that Murrow and Friendly would eventually address McCarthyism on a telecast of the program. On March 8, 1953, *See It Now* made its third and most direct pass at Senator McCarthy. This broadcast was devoted to McCarthy's questioning of Reed Harris, the director of the Voice of America, during the sensational hearings that the senator was at that time conducting. Presented without interruption, Murrow summed it up, dryly, as "an example of investigatory technique." This footage, shown here in its entirety, would become a portion of the program "A Report on Senator McCarthy" that was broadcast one year later. Finally, in late October 1953, the *See It Now* team took on the question of the political and social phenomenon of McCarthyism directly. They broadcast "The Case of Milo Radulovich," a program that centered on the story of a young lieutenant in the Air Force Reserve. For Murrow and Friendly, "Milo Radulovich" was a story representative of the effects of "McCarthyism" and the question of the blacklist and guilt by association. "The Case of Milo Radulovich" was followed one month later by "An Argument in Indianapolis," which examined the suspicion and fear attendant on anything "controversial." Then, in four months "A Report on Senator McCarthy," which focused on the man at the center of the movement, and finally "Annie Lee Moss Before the McCarthy Committee," a program that scrutinized the typical abuses of the congressional investigations that fueled McCarthyism's most sensational publicity coups. "Annie Lee Moss" followed only one week after "Report." These programs—this direct assault on McCarthyism, including the blacklist, the fear of groups labeled "subversive," the tactics of the senator himself, and the abuse of the congressional investigation—consolidated *See It Now*'s position as one of the most heroic moments in the history of journalism and of television broadcasting.

Certainly, it is significant that Joseph McCarthy's rise to national prominence and *See It Now*'s rising influence coincided with an explosive growth of television in the United States. Where in 1947 only roughly 1 in 100 homes had television receivers, by 1955 nearly 80 in 100 owned at least one receiver. [Historian] Erik Barnouw has discussed the importance of *See It Now*.

> The sequence of *See It Now* programs on McCarthyism had extraordinary impact. They placed Murrow in the forefront of the documentary film movement; he was hailed as its television pioneer. . . . Coming at the same time as the finest of the anthology programs, the Murrow documentaries helped to make television an indispensable medium. Few people now dared to be without a television set, and few major advertisers dared to be unrepresented on the home screen. . . . Murrow and the others popularized the medium.

The *See It Now* telecasts, we should keep in mind, are situated at the locus of intersecting historical forces. One vector is, as we have seen, the familiar one of the era of the Red Scare with its blacklists, its guilt-by-association, its sensational spy stories. But another equally significant vector, as we have also seen, involves a more specific threat to the freedoms of the new media institutions. Born in the midst of the era of McCarthyism, the television industry was necessarily shaped by the intimidation associated with that era. Thus, in one way, the *See It Now* series on McCarthyism represents a second and parallel context: the television industry moving against the increasing threat of McCarthyism's domination. As is evident from the particular historical circumstances that surround the *See It Now* programs, each in some way responded to the senator's direct or implied threats; each can be understood as a counter or limit to McCarthyism's circumscription of the topic and treatment of current events.

The Red Scare Damaged American Education

David Caute

Throughout the Red Scare, teachers at every level in the United States were a prime target of suspicion. Few other professions had as much access to and influence over American children and young adults as education; therefore, many anti-Communists believed that educators must be monitored more closely than any other group to prevent Communist influence from corrupting generations of impressionable American students. In this excerpt from his wide-ranging study of American anticommunism, *The Great Fear*, British author and cultural historian David Caute chronicles some of the effects of anticommunism on teachers in the United States, not only during the Red Scare of the Cold War era, but also dating back to the first outburst of anti-Communist sentiment in the 1910s and 1920s. Caute concludes that the Red Scare was disastrous not simply because it expelled so many teachers—rightly or wrongly—from the classroom on suspicion of Communist sympathies, but also because it created an atmosphere of fear and distrust that stifled the expression of thought in the classroom.

The American teaching profession has almost invariably stood exposed as a target for suspicion and aggression at times of superpatriotic sensitivity. During the First World War quite a few professors suspected of pacifism or pro-German

David Caute, *The Great Fear: The Anti-Communist Purge Under Truman and Eisenhower.* New York: Simon and Schuster, 1978. Copyright © 1978 by David Caute. All rights reserved. Reproduced by permission of Georges Borchardt, Inc.

sentiment were shown the door. Between 1917 and 1923, charges of disloyalty were leveled against teachers in thirteen states; teachers were actually fired in eight. Such was the fear during the [1919] "Red Scare"—[President Warren G.] Harding's Commissioner of Education declared his intention of eliminating "Communism, Bolshevism, and Socialism" from schools—that the American Federation of Teachers [AFT] lost about half of its 10,000 members.

By 1940 twenty-one states had introduced loyalty oaths for teachers. From 1942 to 1946 there was a hiatus in oath incantations (America being temporarily allied to the devil) followed by five or six frantic years during which a further fifteen states plunged into loyalty legislation, even though the conservative National Education Association unanimously condemned oaths designed exclusively for teachers. Indeed, in some areas additional affirmations were required by local school boards. Six states specifically barred teachers who belonged to the CP [Communist Party], but the Kansas oath was more typical:

> I,———, swear [or affirm] that I do not advocate, nor am I a member of any political party or organization that advocates the overthrow of the government of the United States or of the State by force or violence. . . .

Thirteen states imposed on teachers oaths explicitly disclaiming membership of a list of organizations usually based on the Attorney General's list, but sometimes garnishing it.

The Effect of the Red Scare in Higher Education

Pressures on colleges and schools tended to be implicit when federal, explicit when locally instigated; although explicit enough was HUAC's [House Committee on Un-American Activities] letter of June 1949 to eighty-one colleges and high schools, demanding lists of textbooks in use in the fields of literature, economics, government, history, political science, social science and geography. The military authorities demanded the right to scrutinize the curricula of about two hundred colleges engaged in classified work under military contract; in 1953 fourteen of forty-six universities refused to renew their contracts with the U.S. Armed Forces Institute because it added a clause endowing itself with the power to veto faculty members conducting correspondence courses under the scheme.

Schools and colleges were governed very rarely by educators, but more commonly by businessmen, bankers, lawyers and, in the case of state universities, by politicians. By 1950 such people accounted for about 80 percent of university trustees or regents. For example, the trustees of the University of Washington at the time of the 1948–49 purge were seven in number: two attorneys, two major industrialists, an investment broker, the corrupt vice-president of the Teamsters [a major labor union], Dave Beck—and a solitary liberal educator. The Board of Regents of the University of California at the time of the loyalty-oath calamity included an osteopath who specialized in property deals, a lawyer who sold his interest in a gold mine for $325,000, two prominent members of Associated Farmers employing sweated Mexican labor and the president of the largest bank in the world, the Bank of America, who declared, "I feel sincerely that if we rescind this oath flags will fly in the Kremlin."

Whereas in Britain the universities have been carefully shielded from transitory public pressures, the heads of American colleges have had to face the rude winds of populist intolerance. A statement put out in March 1953 by the Association of American Universities indicated acquiescense: "The state university is supported by public funds. The endowed university is benefited by tax exemptions. Such benefits are conferred upon universities not as favors but in furtherance of the public interest." While most heads of colleges paid pious lip service to "free, untrammeled research and intellectual speculation," almost all were agreed, like President James B. Conant of Harvard, that CP members were "out of bounds as members of the teaching profession." A distinguished liberal, Mrs. Millicent McIntosh, president of Barnard [College], explained: "If the colleges take the responsibility to do their own house cleaning, Congress would not feel it has to investigate."

Across the country universities barred controversial speakers; in 1955 the University of Washington distinguished itself by banning an address by J. Robert Oppenheimer [the onetime head of the project that created the atomic bomb]. Under Superintendent Hobart M. Corning the District of Columbia school system made a practice of embargoing speakers listed by HCUA, and of submitting names to the Committee for clearance.

The professors and teachers themselves suffered from lack or tenure, low salaries, low status. More than half of American teachers lacked any kind of tenure protection, and only 60,000 out of one million were bold enough to join the American Federation of Teachers. In 1954–55 the average secondary-school teacher was earning $4,194, compared to the automobile worker's wage of $4,947. Indeed the average of assistant professors was also lower than that of automobile workers. Nothing wrong with that; but, whereas in Europe low-paid professionals can enjoy a high status and the self-confidence that goes with it, in America money has tended to operate as the indicator of public esteem. In short, here was a profession it was all too easy to bully and browbeat.

Not surprisingly, the profession bent its knee to the *Zeitgeist* [German word meaning "spirit of the time"]. The National Education Association, with 425,000 members and 800,000 affiliates, declared in June 1949 that CP members had surrendered the right to think for themselves and therefore the right to teach. [New York University] Professor Sidney Hook's influential discourses on this subject—he was short of evidence that Communist teachers actually indoctrinated their pupils, but argued deductively from a few dated Party texts—were thus accepted. It was in 1952 that the AFT resolved not to defend any teacher proven to be a Communist, or who refused to deny that he was one. Only the American Association of University Professors attempted to combat political discrimination in education.

The political purges that hit American colleges and schools during the Truman-Eisenhower era cost at least six hundred, and probably more, teachers and professors their jobs, about

380 of them in New York City. The scale of intimidation was partly reflected in a survey conducted in 1955 of 2,451 social-science teachers, in 165 colleges and universities, who reported 386 incidents involving allegations of Communism, subversion or fellow-traveling, 10 percent of which resulted in dismissal or forced resignation. In a further 108 cases involving charges of "leftist" political sympathies or activities (almost invariably sympathies), no fewer than 16 percent culminated in dismissal or forced resignation. . . .

Fear in the Schools

As Robert M. Hutchins was to put it, "The question is not how many teachers have been fired, but how many think they might be, and for what reasons. . . . The entire teaching profession of the U.S. is now intimidated." Despite a 5 to 1 protest by the faculty, the University of Wyoming went ahead with an examination of hundreds of its textbooks for subversive or un-American material. Surveying seventy-two major colleges in the early part of 1951, [New York Times writer] Kalman Siegel reported "a subtle, creeping paralysis of freedom of thought and speech" and "a narrowing of the area of tolerance." Two years later Time magazine, somewhat tardily noticing "The Danger Signals," cited a wide variety of distinguished academics whose alarm could not be attributed to camouflaged radicalism. Robert Bolwell, professor of American literature at George Washington University, commented: "I confess that after finishing a lecture, I sometimes wonder if somebody is going to take it to Papa or to some reporter. . . . One lecture could damn anybody." Dean Carl W. Ackerman, of the Columbia University Graduate School of Journalism, said, "Today the vast majority of teachers . . . have learned that promotion and security depend upon conformity to the prevailing . . . concept of devotion to the public welfare."

The Lazarsfeld study, based on 2,451 interviews conducted in 165 colleges in 1955, revealed that 63 percent of the social scientists interviewed believed the threat to intellectual activity was greater than a generation before. Only 16 percent of the incidents recorded by the respondents had to do with anything so specific as Party membership or invocation of the Fifth Amendment; the great majority—84 percent—reflected the nebulous, pervasive concern with "sympathizers," "subversives," "un-Americans." No fewer than 365 respondents had been offered advice by colleagues on how to avoid political trouble on campus. Courses on Soviet economics, et cetera, were liable to cause comment, to be vetted by administration officials, to be toned down, to be canceled. Fear of recommending radical reading material paralleled fear of student informers; more than half reported that one colleague or another had been accused of subversive sympathies. The effect of this climate on the content and tone of American sociological writing lies beyond the scope of this study; yet it is surely no coincidence that it was at this time that the "discovery" was made that "left" and "right" were no longer political terms of any relevance; and that the productive, quantitative triumphs of managerial-capitalist society had rendered the whole concept of ideology obsolete. The [1950s] were coated in chromium [i.e, covered with a shiny finish that disguised their true nature].

How a Loyalty Oath Almost Ruined a University

Dan Fowler

In 1949, the University of California at Berkeley decided to require all of its employees to sign an oath that
explicitly stated their opposition to communism. This
decision prompted a three-year process of protests, negotia-
tions, firings, and reconciliations that is chronicled in this
article by Dan Fowler from the January 29, 1952, issue of
Look magazine. Fowler begins by pointing out that the original oath was not intended to identify Communists on the
Berkeley campus but had been a public-relations move to
ensure continued public funding for the university. When a
number of high-profile faculty members objected that the
oath resembled the tactics adopted by totalitarian governments such as Nazi Germany, a battle of wills ensued between a substantial group of faculty members who refused
to sign the oath and the board of regents, the main adminis-
trative body of the university. Fowler argues that the issues
surrounding the loyalty oath had as much to do with campus politics as a genuine desire to root out Communists. He
also contends that the loyalty oath almost succeeded at destroying the very institution that it had set out to protect.

Three years ago [in 1949], the regents of the University of
California forced their faculty members to take oaths
denying that they were Communists. A group of teachers refused to sign, precipitating a bitter academic conflict which is

Dan Fowler, "What the Loyalty Oath Did to the University of California," *Look*, vol.
16, January 29, 1952, pp. 50–52. Copyright © 1952 by Cowles Broadcasting, Inc.
Reproduced by permission.

just now being resolved. The affair furnishes a good case history on fear-inspired oath-taking.

The imposition of the oath had these results:

The university lost directly—by firing, protest resignations or refusal of appointments—more than 100 scholars, including some widely described as "among the illustrious minds of our generation."

The university was forced to drop 55 courses from its curriculum for lack of instructors. Entire departments were crippled.

The university lost an enormous amount of professional prestige. Some 1,200 members of the faculties of 40 other colleges and universities condemned the action. Twenty-three illustrious learned societies condemned the loyalty oath and recommended that their members refuse appointments at California.

In short, the action of the regents followed the pattern of hysteria-induced actions—it came dangerously close to destroying the thing it was supposed to save.

Great Results

And from all this wreckage of reputation, morale and intellectual power were dredged exactly two people who could be labeled as Communists. One was a piano player employed in dancing classes. The other was a part-time graduate student working as a teaching assistant.

The avowed purpose of the oath was to root Reds and Red influences out of the California faculty. The suspicion naturally followed that there must be a great many Communists among the faculty to justify such action. This suspicion, vigorously fanned by a few ambitious state politicians, greatly damaged the university's fine reputations.

Within the institution itself, the results were even worse. Members of the faculty were forced to meet secretly, suspect each other, examine each others' records and motives and even censor their own telephone conversations on the campus.

Ironically, the University of California's loyalty oath was never even intended to be the weapon for ousting Reds which it was advertised to be. It was, actually, a device by which the school's administration hoped to preserve its appropriations in lobbying before the legislature.

The University of California loyalty oath dates back to 1948 and to Jack Tenney, then a state assemblyman. Tenney was a politician who rode to the office on a program of fear psychology and he introduced a broadside of anti-subversive bills in the legislature. One of these bills would have required a loyalty oath from the faculty of the University, although its disloyalty never had been proved nor even seriously questioned.

Since the legislature controls the school's appropriations the university's lobbyist became fearful that Tenney's move might affect the amount of revenue. He decided that the wisest course would be to beat Tenney to the punch. President Robert G. Sproul agreed with this reasoning and the university's own loyalty oath—not one adopted by the legislature—was drawn up and on Sproul's recommendations was adopted by the regents on March 25, 1989.

So the oath was born. Not to combat communism. Just to protect the university's source of revenue.

One obvious question which became a political issue and a subject of great newspaper comment was this:

"Why should any patriotic American—if he has nothing to hide—object to taking an oath that he is not a Communist?"

It seems a reasonable question to many people, but the faculty members who objected to it insisted they had reasonable answers.

Unjustified Aspersion

Originally, when it still masqueraded in a cloak of anti-Communist respectability, the oath was resented by faculty members as a completely unjustified reflection on their loyalty and integrity. One retort colorfully expressed this resentment. "We'll deny we are a subversive group," it ran, "if the regents will take an oath that they are not homosexuals." The meaning is clear: Compel any group, however respectable, to swear that it is *not* something and suspicion is born that it is—where there's smoke there's fire, etc., etc.

Some of the teachers maintained that the oath of allegiance to the constitutions of the United States and the State of California signed by all faculty members when they entered the university, was oath enough. They argued that any Communist who would take these oaths of allegiance would be the first to sign any additional oath: that instead of trapping any real Communist the new oath would serve only to conceal him better.

Opposition to signing the loyalty oath was led by Edward C. Tolman, former professor of psychology at California, considered one of the country's foremost psychologists. Among his many honors is a doctorate bestowed by Yale University after he refused to sign the oath and left the university. He is now here [at Yale] writing a book.

Another leader of this group was Professor Ernst H. Kantorowicz, a political refugee from Nazi Germany and distinguished historian now a member of the Institute for Advanced Study at Princeton.

"This is the way it always begins," he warned a faculty meeting. "The first oath is so gentle you can scarcely notice anything at which to take exception. The next oath is stronger. The first oath demanded of German teachers by Hitler was to keep faith with the Fatherland and to honor the constitution and laws. But the next," he reminded his colleagues, "demanded allegiance to Adolf Hitler." . . .

Thus, the principle of academic freedom was injected into the controversy. Although it is perhaps not too well understood outside the teaching profession, academic freedom is a precious thing to educators. In its most idealistic meaning, academic freedom is complete freedom to seek and teach the truth. It means to a bio-chemist, for example, freedom to prove that some nostrum is harmful without fear of reprisals by the manufacturer. To a professor it means freedom to think and talk and write without political pressure or attempts to have him discharged.

Finally, the oath was supposed by those who believed that keeping the university free of Reds was the faculty's job and not the regents. And the question raised by this opposition, "Who's running this university, the faculty or the regents?" became the real battle line in the three-year fight.

Pulled a Gun

Angered by a challenge to its power, the regents pulled a gun. "Sign or get out," they told the faculty, in effect. And, as happens when a gun is drawn, the regents were forced either to use it or back down.

The showdown came when in a last attempt to settle the dispute a committee of alumni was authorized to seek a compromise. In an effort to appraise both sides, the alumni group worked out a plan whereby faculty employment contracts would contain a non-Communist statement. Then a clause was added to the contract giving non-signers the right to a hearing before the faculty's Committee on Privilege and Tenure. Although the regents previously had accepted recommendations of this committee, they inserted a clause of their own into the compromise: "It is recognized that final determination of each case is the prerogative of the regents."

Forty-nine faculty members refused to sign the non-Communist contracts and appeared before the Tenure Committee for hearings. Six refused to answer questions and their discharge was recommended—not, of course, because they were Communists but because they refused to live up to the terms of the compromise agreement worked out by the alumni committee.

The other 43 non-signers spent four weeks testifying before the committee and their retention on the faculty was strongly recommended. A transcript of their testimony was delivered to the regents along with this statement:

"It is this committee's deliberate judgement that the refusal of non-signers as a group to accept the contract of employment is not based upon sympathy with communism as an active and destructive force but upon a variety of opinions and feelings which have no relation to resolution or destruction of any kind. They are valuable members of the university faculty."

Previous Screening

The committee report also included testimony showing that 26 of the non-signers had previously been screened by Federal Bureau of Investigation agents or Army authorities and cleared for war or defense work.

To clarify its position, the faculty adopted a policy statement opposing the hiring of Communists as teachers. And at a regents' meeting which considered the faculty committee recommendations the question of communism was once more disposed of. C.J. Haggerty, an anti-oath regent, declared, "There is no longer an impugning of these individuals (the non-signers) as Communists." To which Governor Earl Warren, also an anti-oath regent, added: "We are discharging these people because they are recalcitrant and won't conform." According to those present, the pro-oath regents also agreed that communism was no longer an issue, that the only issue was discipline. Thus, the fight had gone from its original framework.

The first vote on the committee's recommendations was in favor of re-instating those who testified but refused to sign. But advocates of the oath, led by John F. Neylan, a regent, delayed final action to the next meeting, mustered their forces and fired the non-signers by a two-vote margin.

They had used their gun to prove who was running the university. They were.

At this point the Board of Regents appeared in a rather awkward position. They had committed themselves to a policy of "Let's give them a fair trial and then hang 'em." And they had fired—for refusing to sign a statement that they were not Communists—men who had been officially screened and found completely free of taint.

Tenure Violated

But that wasn't all. When they refused to renew the contracts of those who would not sign the non-Communist statement they violated academic tenure.

Academic tenure is the thing which guarantees academic freedom in a university; in some it is a written guarantee. It is a respected tradition that a faculty member cannot be discharged except for proved incompetence or moral turpitude. This is the professor's guarantee of security, his assurance of the kind of life for which a fine scientist will pass up a high-salaried post in industry for a lifetime of classroom and research.

The violation of this principle at the University of California brought the full weight of America's academic world down on the regents' heads.

Robert Penn Warren, now at Yale, a Pulitzer Prize winner, the author of *All the King's Men,* declared in declining an offer to teach at California, "It seems to me that the regents of the University of California would reduce the academic community, both faculty and administration, to the level of hired hands serving at the whim of a group of men whose acquaintance with intellectual life and its responsibilities is, in some cases at least, of the most rudimentary order."

Rudolph Carnap of the University of Chicago, regarded as one of the three leading philosophers alive today, wrote, "I regard the peremptory dismissal of eminent scholars, without regard to their tenure rights and their long-distinguished service to the university, as a shocking violation of academic freedom. I wish my refusal to accept any honor from this university to be regarded as a protest against the violation of the principle that scholarship, teaching ability and integrity of character should be the only criteria for judging a man's fitness for an academic position."

Howard Mumford Jones, Harvard English professor and poet, playwright and author of distinctions as well as scholar, declined an invitation from California as follows: "Until your board of regents ceases to violate the ordinary principles of academic tenure and honest agreement between parties to a contract, I cannot in good conscience accept." . . .

Court Invalidation

The regents' vote which crammed the oath down the faculty's throat subsequently was held by a California Appeals court to be unconstitutional and invalid.

In attempting to justify their action, regents who approved the oath maintained (and still do) that they possessed power

to fire any faculty members and were not bound by law to follow any committee's recommendations even after they implic-
itly agreed to honor faculty recommendations when they
adopted the alumni compromise.

In further defense of their action, some pro-oath regents
have made much of the fact that an overwhelming majority of
faculty members signed the non-Communist contracts. They
blame the whole thing on "a dissident minority," the handful
of non-signers.

This defense is weak, for in every role in which the oath issue
was clearly drawn, the faculty condemned it and the list of those
who signed under protest is lengthy. Also, a "sign, stay and
fight" movement developed which encouraged many to sign.

What, then, brought about this remarkable vote?

It has been charged that politicians among the regents sought
to embarrass Governor Warren, who fought the oath as un-
lawful and impractical from the beginning. It was blamed on
another group "out to get" President Sproul for getting them
into the mess and then changing his mind. And it was blamed
on a third faction out to get Sproul because he stands for university unity while they favor greater autonomy for the University of California at the Los Angeles campus.

All of these things may have influenced the vote, but the
best guess would be that the pro-oath faction, angered and determined to show who was boss, maneuvered themselves into
an impossible position and wouldn't admit it.

Nearly Over

This case history in oaths is almost ended. The appeals court
which declared the oath unconstitutional has ordered rein-
statement of the non-signers.

The complexion of the Board of Regents has changed. Term
expirations depleted the old majority and Governor Warren
has replaced pro-oath regents with men who share his view.
The November, 1951, meeting of the board finally rescinded it
officially.

In doing so, the new majority did save face for the old
guard: It held that a recent legislative act compelling all state

employees to take non-Communist oaths had made the special regents oath unnecessary. Despite this hedge, the new majority seems firmly dedicated to the theory that the faculty is best suited to settle faculty problems.

A certain atmosphere of suspicion and distrust is bound to overhang this great school for a time, but the general feeling now is one of optimism. Academic tenure seems secure again. Sproul, who admitted the oath was a mistake and changed belatedly to the faculty's side, appears to be as strong as ever. After this trial, the university which split the atom, produced six Nobel Prize winners, and has many other notable achievements, seems strong and well. The court which held the regents' oath invalid declared:

"We are keenly aware that, equal to the danger of subversion from within by force and violence, is the danger of subversion from within by the gradual whittling away and the resulting disintegration of the very pillars of our freedom."

▓ CHRONOLOGY

1905

June: The International Workers of the World (IWW) union is founded in Chicago.

1912

November: Socialist Party candidate Eugene V. Debs receives 6 percent of the popular vote in the U.S. presidential election, the most ever for a Socialist candidate.

1917

March 8: The Romanov dynasty is overthrown in Russia by a coalition of leftist revolutionary groups. By November the Bolshevik faction of the Communist Party seizes full political control and establishes the Soviet Union in 1922 after five years of civil war.

June 15: Congress passes the Espionage Act, making it illegal to interfere with the operation of the U.S. military or to aid its enemies. The law is publicly applied in July, when it is used to justify the suppression of an IWW-supported strike of miners in Bisbee, Arizona.

1918

May 16: Congress passes the Sedition Act, forbidding the use of "disloyal, profane, scurrilous, or abusive language" by Americans. Under this law the postmaster general is empowered to stop or delay the delivery of potentially seditious material, which includes almost all Socialist and Communist mailings.

November: Despite being under indictment for supposed espionage, Victor L. Berger of Wisconsin is elected to the U.S. House of Representatives as a member of the Socialist Party. Congress refuses to seat him until 1921, when the charges against him are dismissed by the Supreme Court.

1919

May–October: Tensions between radical labor groups and reactionaries intensify in a series of street clashes, high-profile strikes, and bombings.

November 7: The so-called "Palmer Raids" begin, by the order of Attorney General A. Mitchell Palmer. Over the course of the next year tens of thousands of alleged Communists are arrested and/or deported.

1920

May 5: Two anarchists, Nicola Sacco and Bartolomeo Vanzetti, are arrested in connection with a robbery and murder in Boston. They are convicted in a highly politicized trial and become a cause célèbre that long survives their execution in 1927.

September 16: A bomb explodes in New York's Wall Street financial district, killing thirty-nine people and injuring more than four hundred. The explosion triggers another round of reprisals against leftist radicals.

1921

March 3: Parts of the Espionage Act of 1917 and all of the Sedition Act of 1918 are repealed.

1924

May 10: J. Edgar Hoover is appointed director of the Federal Bureau of Investigation, a post he will hold until 1972.

1929

October: The U.S. stock market loses nearly 40 percent of its value during the month, triggering a widespread economic crisis known as the Great Depression, which lasts for most of the 1930s. During this time Communist and Socialist organizations will reach the height of their influence among American workers, 14 million of whom will be unemployed in 1933.

1930

July–December: A special House of Representatives committee chaired by Hamilton Fish (R-NY) holds hearings on Communist influence in the United States. Its recommendations that the Communist Party should be outlawed and Communists should be deported are ultimately rejected.

1932

March: With the organizational assistance of the Communist Party, several thousand unemployed automobile industry workers march on the Ford Motor Company plant in Dearborn, Michigan. Local police open fire on the marchers and kill four men.

1934

Summer–Fall: A special House committee led by Samuel Dickstein (D-NY) and John McCormack (D-MA) investigates allegations of both pro-Nazi and pro-Communist activities in the United States. Several of its recommendations will become part of the Smith Act of 1940.

1938

August: The special House Select Committee on Un-American Activities, chaired by Martin Dies (D-TX), convenes to investigate subversive activities. It will continue to operate off and on until Dies's retirement in 1944.

1940

June: Congress passes the Alien Registration Act (also known as the Smith Act), which not only requires the registration and fingerprinting of all foreigners living in the United States but also makes it a crime to advocate the overthrow of the U.S. government.

1945

January 3: The House Committee on Un-American Activities (HUAC) becomes a standing, or permanent, committee, charged with investigating propaganda and other subversive activities by individuals and groups hostile to the United States.

September 2: World War II ends, and the wartime alliance with the Soviet Union soon collapses.

1946

March 5: Former British prime minister Winston Churchill gives his "Iron Curtain" speech in Fulton, Missouri. For many this speech marks the start of the Cold War.

1947

October 20: HUAC begins hearings investigating Communist infiltration of the motion picture industry in Hollywood.

November 24: The "Hollywood Ten" are cited with contempt of Congress for their refusal to cooperate with HUAC. They are "blacklisted" by all the major motion picture studios the next day.

1949

March 25: The University of California institutes a loyalty oath for all its faculty and staff.

May: State Department official Alger Hiss is tried on perjury charges related to accusations of espionage made against him by Whittaker Chambers. The first trial ends in a hung jury, but Hiss is eventually found guilty in a second trial that ends on January 21, 1950.

August 29: The Soviet Union tests its first atomic bomb near Semipalatinsk, Kazakhstan.

September 4: A Communist-sponsored concert featuring noted performer Paul Robeson in Peekskill, New York, ends with concertgoers being attacked by anti-Communists and police.

October 1: The People's Republic of China is founded.

1950

February 3: Physicist Klaus Fuchs admits to passing secrets related to the atomic bomb to Soviet agents.

February 9: In a speech in Wheeling, West Virginia, Senator Joseph McCarthy (R-WI) claims to have a list of "known Communists" working in the State Department.

March 29: The term "McCarthyism" is first used by *Washington Post* editorial cartoonist Herbert Block.

Spring: The "Committee for the Present Danger" is founded by a group of prominent intellectuals to spread information about the dangers of communism.

June 25: The Korean War begins.

July: A Senate committee headed by Millard Tydings (D-MD) rejects McCarthy's claims of Communist infiltration of the U.S. government.

July 17: Julius Rosenberg is arrested on suspicion of espionage in relation to the atomic bomb. His wife Ethel is arrested on August 11.

September: Congress passes the Internal Security Act (also known as the McCarran Act), which requires all Communists and Communist-allied organizations to register with the U.S. attorney general's office. It also creates the Senate Internal Security Subcommittee, the counterpart to HUAC.

1951

March 21: HUAC begins a second round of hearings on communism in the entertainment industry.

March 29: Julius and Ethel Rosenberg are convicted of conspiracy to commit espionage. A week later they are sentenced to death by electrocution.

1952

January: Congress passes the McCarran-Walter Act, allowing deportation of any foreigners or naturalized American citizens who are convicted of subversive acts.

1953

January 22: Arthur Miller's play *The Crucible* premieres in New York.

Spring: The Senate Permanent Subcommittee on Investigations, chaired by McCarthy, begins televised hearings investigating suspected Communist infiltration of the government and the military.

June 19: Julius and Ethel Rosenberg are executed as Soviet nuclear spies.

July 27: The Korean War ends.

1954

May 27: Manhattan Project leader J. Robert Oppenheimer has his top-secret security clearance revoked after being accused of Communist sympathies.

June 9: During televised hearings into the alleged presence of Communists in the army, lawyer Joseph Welch publicly rebukes McCarthy with the famous phrase "Have you no decency, sir, at long last?"

December 2: McCarthy is censured by the Senate, effectively ending his influence.

1956

The FBI initiates its secret Counter-Intelligence Program (COINTELPRO), which operates covertly over the next fifteen years to gather information about groups and individuals in the United States suspected of subversive activity.

1957

May 2: McCarthy dies.

May 31: Miller is convicted of contempt of Congress when he refuses to cooperate with a HUAC investigation. The charges are dismissed more than a year later.

October 4: The Soviet Union launches *Sputnik,* the first artificial satellite in Earth orbit.

1958

December: The John Birch Society—named after a U.S intelligence officer killed in China in 1945—is founded by industrialist Robert Welch. It soon becomes one of the most influential anti-Communist organizations in the United States.

1972

May 2: J. Edgar Hoover dies. Upon his death, his longtime secretary shreds most of the personal files Hoover kept on individuals and groups over his forty-eight-year tenure as FBI director.

FOR FURTHER RESEARCH

Books

John G. Adams, *Without Precedent: The Story of the Death of McCarthyism.* New York: Norton, 1983.

Paul Avrich, *Sacco and Vanzetti: The Anarchist Background.* Princeton, NJ: Princeton University Press, 1991.

Michael Barson, *Red Scared! The Commie Menace in Propaganda and Popular Culture.* San Francisco: Chronicle, 2001.

Jonathan Bell, *The Liberal State on Trial: The Cold War and American Politics in the Truman Years.* New York: Columbia University Press, 2004.

Eric Bentley, ed., *Thirty Years of Treason: Excerpts from Hearings Before the House Committee on Un-American Activities, 1938–1968.* New York: Nation, 2001.

Paul Buhle and Dave Wagner, *Hide in Plain Sight: The Hollywood Blacklistees in Film and Television, 1950–2002.* New York: Palgrave Macmillan, 2003.

Roy Cohn, *McCarthy.* New York: New American Library, 1968.

Richard M. Fried, *Nightmare in Red: The McCarthy Era in Perspective.* New York: Oxford University Press, 1990.

Robert Griffith, *The Politics of Fear: Joseph R. McCarthy and the Senate.* Lexington: University of Kentucky Press, 1970.

David Halberstam, *The Fifties.* New York: Villard, 1993.

Harvey Klehr and John Earl Haynes, *The Secret World of American Communism.* New Haven, CT: Yale University Press, 1995.

Stanley I. Kutler, *The American Inquisition: Justice and Injustice in the Cold War.* New York: Hill and Wang, 1982.

Ring Lardner Jr., *I'd Hate Myself in the Morning*. New York: Nation, 2001.

Earl Latham, *The Communist Controversy in Washington: From the New Deal to McCarthy*. Cambridge, MA: Harvard University Press, 1966.

William Edward Leuchtenburg, *The Perils of Prosperity, 1914–1932*. Chicago: University of Chicago Press, 1993.

David W. McFadden, *Alternative Paths: Soviets and Americans, 1917–1920*. New York: Oxford University Press, 1993.

Victor S. Navasky, *Naming Names*. Revised ed. New York: Hill and Wang, 2003.

Kenneth O'Reilly, *Hoover and the Un-Americans: The FBI, HUAC, and the Red Menace*. Philadelphia: Temple University Press, 1983.

Charles Potter, *Days of Shame*. New York: Coward-McCann, 1965.

Ronald Radosh and Joyce Milton, *The Rosenberg File*. 2nd ed. New Haven, CT: Yale University Press, 1997.

Thomas C. Reeves, *The Life and Times of Joe McCarthy*. New York: Stein and Day, 1982.

Lisle A. Rose, *The Cold War Comes to Main Street: America in 1950*. Lawrence: University Press of Kansas, 1999.

Ellen Schrecker, *Many Are the Crimes: McCarthyism in America*. Princeton, NJ: Princeton University Press, 1999.

Films

Citizen Cohn. Directed by Frank Pierson. HBO Films, 1992.

Guilty by Suspicion. Directed by Irwin Winkler. Warner Brothers, 1991.

High Noon. Directed by Fred Zinnemann. United Artists, 1952.

I Was a Communist for the F.B.I. Directed by Gordon Douglas. Warner Brothers, 1951.

The Manchurian Candidate. Directed by John Frankenheimer. United Artists, 1962.

Web Sites

The American 1950s, www.writing.upenn.edu/~afilreis/50s/ home.html. Developed by Al Filreis, professor of English at the University of Pennsylvania, this site is a clearinghouse of information on the 1950s in general, including numerous materials pertaining directly to the Red Scare. An excellent starting point for research into the period.

CNN: *The Cold War,* Episode 6, www.cnn.com/SPECIALS/ cold.war/episodes/06. The online companion to CNN's popular documentary on the Cold War focuses on issues related to the second Red Scare. The site includes video from the period, transcripts of testimony at the HUAC Hollywood hearings and McCarthy's famous 1950 speech claiming to have a list of Communists in the State Department.

Federal Bureau of Investigation: John Edgar Hoover, www.fbi. gov/libref/directors/hoover.htm. This is a page on the FBI's official Web site devoted to its longest-serving director—the man for whom the building in which the FBI currently resides is named. The page includes a brief biography of Hoover, a photograph of him early in his career, and links to other material about the institution he controlled for nearly fifty years.

Red Scare, 1918–1921: An Image Database, http://newman. baruch.cuny.edu/digital/redscare. Created by librarian Leo R. Klein, this is a searchable database of images—photographs, scans of pamphlets, editorial cartoons—and texts relating to the first Red Scare. As such, it provides an invaluable look at the ways in which American culture responded to the perceived threat of communism in the wake of the Russian Revolution.